EVERY NIGHT
ITALIAN

120 SIMPLE, DELICIOUS RECIPES YOU CAN PREPARE IN 45 MINUTES OR LESS

Giuliano Hazan

Color Photographs by Dana Gallagher
Illustrations by Glenn Wolff

Foreword by Marcella Hazan

SCRIBNER
NEW YORK LONDON SYDNEY SINGAPORE

SCRIBNER
1230 Avenue of the Americas
New York, NY 10020

Text copyright © 2000 by Giuliano Hazan
Photographs copyright © 2000 by Dana Gallagher
Illustrations copyright © 2000 by Glenn Wolff

All rights reserved, including the right of reproduction in whole or in part in any form.

SCRIBNER and design are trademarks of Macmillan Library Reference USA,
Inc., used under license by Simon & Schuster, the publisher of this work.

DESIGNED BY BRITTA STEINBRECHT

Set in Hoefler Text and News Gothic

Manufactured in the United States of America

1 3 5 7 9 10 8 6 4 2

Library of Congress Cataloging-in-Publication Dataa
Hazan, Giuliano.
Every night Italian : 120 simple, delicious recipes you can prepare
in 45 minutes or less / Giuliano Hazan.
p. cm.
Includes index.
1. Cookery, Italian.   2. Quick and easy cookery. I. Title.
TX723 .H334 2000
641.5945—dc21   99-37394
CIP

ISBN 0-684-80028-4

For Lael,

my wife, my partner, my love

Contents

Acknowledgments

IN ALL MY RESEARCH trips, countless people generously gave of their time and knowledge to assist me and I am very grateful to all of them. I would like to give special thanks to the following people:

My wife, Lael, for her constant support—cheering me on or nudging me as needed—for her discriminating palate, for her sense of humor, and for putting up with dinners that sometimes consisted of the same dish made five different ways, as well as for the many hours she spent reading and commenting on my manuscript. Her ability to put herself in the place of my readers has been invaluable.

I am very lucky to have Maria Guarnaschelli as my editor. Her boundless enthusiasm, attention to detail, and extraordinary vision have been invaluable in creating this book.

Susan Lescher, my agent and friend, for her guidance and encouragement, and for always being there when I needed her.

Nanette and Giuseppe Galloni, for their insight into Sicilian cooking and their unceasing support and appreciation of my work.

Diane Haglund and Charlie Jimenez, my travel companions on a research trip to Italy, for always letting me order for them at the restaurants we visited.

Bill Malloy, for being so generous in giving of his time and talents.

And, of course, my parents, Victor and Marcella Hazan, for giving me the taste memories that help me define Italian cooking, for sharing their love of food with me, and for supporting me in all my endeavors.

Foreword

ENCOURAGED BY THE POPULARITY of his first cookbook, *The Classic Pasta Cookbook*, my son, Giuliano, announced that he would start work on another. "Have you got a particular approach in mind yet?" I asked him. "I do," he said. "Whenever I chat with the people who have come to one of my cooking classes, and I ask them what they cook every day at home, they say they don't have time to cook every day. When they entertain or on long weekends, but never every day. Don't you find that peculiar, Mother? All over Italy, at each mealtime, families come home to freshly cooked food. Women have jobs and careers, just as they do in America, yet they, and many men, too, manage to prepare a tasty meal every day. I'd like to show Americans how it can be done."

Admittedly, Italian lives play out to a different rhythm than American ones. Most of that country shuts down for a few hours at midday so that people can leave their work to have their main meal at home. Rare is the neighborhood that doesn't have either market stalls or excellent food shops, and one doesn't have far to go for fresh, local ingredients and basic staples. It's unrealistic to try to graft Italian life onto American roots. But some of the values that bring richness and stability to Italian families can do the same for a family in this country, whether dinner is at noontime, as it is in Italy and as it was once in America's South, or in the evening, as it is throughout America today. Those values are engendered and reaffirmed at the moment when the family, be it large or small, can come to the table expecting to share and enjoy good food.

How to find the time? Giuliano shows you how you can put a delicious, heartwarming dinner on the table in less than an hour, as so many Italians do. No one, I think, is better qualified than he to interpret the genuine, life-enhancing flavor of Italian food so that a hurried and harried American cook can confidently and regularly reproduce it. One doesn't choose to transmit a culinary tradition from one culture to another simply because one wants to, but because one can. Although American-born, Giuliano was raised not just in an Italian home but in an Italian kitchen. He lived some of his most formative years in Italy, a country to which he returns each year. At the same time, with his California-born wife, he is bringing up his own young American family in a very American place, a medium-size town on the west coast of Florida. He knows what you need to know because for him it's not theory, it's practice. It's the food that he puts on *his* family table every day.

Now that my husband and I have transplanted ourselves from Italy to the States, and I too have become an American housewife, I intend to profit from Giuliano's experiences. There are so many dishes in this marvelous book that I shall be making for my husband: the Soup with Mushrooms and Potatoes, the Fusilli with Cauliflower and Olives, the Fish with Juniper, and the Braised Beef are among them. I have had the Orange Tart at Giuliano's house and if mine turns out half as well as his, it is likely to become our favorite dessert.

Every Night Italian is a glorious promise, and I congratulate Giuliano on his daring to make it. It is not just a way of cooking but also—through cooking—a way of living. It is a way that has brought and continues to bring happiness to millions. When you buy Giuliano's book, it will assuredly make him happy. But when you use it and act upon its premise, it should make you happy. I hope it shall.

Marcella Hazan

Introduction

BREATHTAKINGLY DELICIOUS, dish after dish—stunningly quick, with only three or four basic ingredients and easy techniques—*Every Night Italian* is an absolute treasure for busy cooks.

Giuliano Hazan is a second-generation chef and an outstanding teacher and writer with an intense love of fine food and wine from both his famous mother, Marcella Hazan, and his wine expert father, Victor. From this rich heritage Giuliano has intensified the best of the best.

He has surpassed even his mother's great talent for creating wonderful taste with few ingredients. His Shrimp Broiled with Rosemary (Gamberoni al Forno) contains basic ingredients—olive oil, lemon juice, salt, pepper, and rosemary—and a quick technique for deveining shrimp without peeling them. Literally in minutes you have prepared a magnificent dish from a famous Italian restaurant.

Giuliano has been executive chef in fine restaurants and is a master of classic techniques, but he is an even greater master of simplifying preparations. He has the kind of expertise that comes only from years of experience.

Marcella tells of sending Giuliano to summer camp when he was about seven years old. The supervisor explained that each camper would have a job, so they should be ready by the end of the week to select an activity that they liked and would like to help with. This might be putting up the canoes or setting up the archery targets. Giuliano did not wait until the end of the week. The second day he went to the supervisor and told him, "I have selected my job. You have to let me cook. I can't eat this food!" And cook he did, for the whole camp.

The writing itself is charming. You will immediately fall in love with Giuliano's straightforward honesty and intense love of good food. I know that *Every Night Italian* will be a much-treasured, grease-spattered mainstay of kitchens around the country.

Shirley O. Corriher

Preface

COOKING HAS FASCINATED ME for as long as I can remember. My mother remembers how, when I was still on my hands and knees, I would amuse myself by opening all the kitchen cabinets I could reach to pull out the pots and pans. One time I found a bottle of olive oil and proceeded to pour it all over myself. Fortunately, I was not banned from the kitchen for long, and whenever my mother cooked, I sat perched on a stool watching, smelling, and tasting. Thus I began to accumulate taste memories and assimilate the instinct for cooking. In fact I probably learned to cook through osmosis.

As I grew older my mother would let me help with certain dishes. Risotto became my specialty; once she had started it, I was entrusted to finish it, stirring constantly and adding just the right amount of liquid when necessary. It was not until I left home, however, that I began cooking in earnest. I missed the food I had grown up with, and the only way for me to eat it was to cook it myself. Whereas many people are motivated to cook for others, for me it was always the prospect of a good meal that made me want to cook (although I certainly take great pleasure in seeing my wife and friends enjoy the dishes I prepare).

I learned to cook because I like to eat well, and I like to eat that way every day, not just on weekends or special occasions. After all, food is a basic human need, so why not make it an enjoyable experience? Mealtimes are also an opportunity for family and friends to be together. Many people tell me they love to cook but don't have the time or are only able to do it occasionally. But cooking does not necessarily mean spending all day in the kitchen. Satisfying food does not have to be complex or take a long time to prepare. Often the simpler it is, the better it tastes, and simplicity is what Italian cooking is all about. It is about clean flavors, enhancing a few fresh ingredients rather than drowning them with heavy sauces and too many spices. Italian food is healthy. Butter and cream are used sparingly, as an accent. Although serving a dish of olive oil with bread for dipping is the latest rage in Italian restaurants in America, in Italy bread is served as an accompaniment to food, and neither butter nor olive oil is needed.

What I hope to accomplish in this book is to make good Italian cooking more accessible so that it can easily become an everyday activity. The key to getting food on the table in a relatively short amount of time is working efficiently in the kitchen. Most of the recipes in this book can be done in forty-five minutes or less. When longer cooking times are required, the preparation is always simple and quick. Often the slow-cooking recipes are dishes that keep well so they can be made in larger batches. In each of my recipes, I guide you as to when to clean, cut, and chop the ingredients you need. I have indicated the approximate time it will take to make each recipe. If it is a dish that needs to cook for a long time I have provided both the preparation time and the total time from start to finish. Naturally, the first time you make a dish it may take a little longer, but once you have made it two or three times the process will be much faster.

What I hope will be a very helpful section in this cookbook is the Menus chapter. With a little bit of planning you can prepare an entire meal in a relatively short amount of time. Cooking several courses does not necessarily take that much longer than making just one dish. All that is necessary is learning how to have more than one dish cooking at a time and coordinating everything to be ready at the right time. I have created "recipes" for complete meals, from simple family dinners to multicourse buffets, with step-by-step instructions for how to prepare each meal from beginning to end.

At our wedding, my wife, Lael, and I wanted to perform a tango as our first dance. We signed up for lessons with an instructor who agreed to help choreograph it for us. At first it was daunting having to remember all the steps and the order in which we were supposed to do them. Once we learned the routine, however, and didn't need to concentrate on where our feet were going, it felt as if we were finally dancing! Preparing a recipe is very similar. The first time you make a dish, you must measure the ingredients and follow instructions and the process can seem tedious and overly time-consuming. But it is actually like learning the steps of a dance. Once you learn the steps, you can let go and enjoy yourself! Ultimately a recipe, no matter how detailed and precise, is only an attempt to crystallize the ever-changing and fluid process that is cooking. Just as it is impossible to step into the same river twice, it is impossible to make a dish exactly the same way twice.

Using the best ingredients and bringing out their flavor is essential to Italian cooking. That is why going to the store is the first step in the process of cooking a meal. Most of the time I don't know what I want to make for dinner until I see what's at the market. I might be thinking of making a veal roast, but the veal that day may not look as good as the beautiful piece of sea bass in the seafood department. Suddenly I have lost my interest in veal roast, and my mouth is watering for grilled sea bass instead. The produce section is another source of inspiration. If the asparagus looks particularly inviting, the zucchini I had in mind may not appeal to me as much. Going to the market every day, although it can be very enjoyable, may not always be practical in our busy lives. Shopping once every two weeks can be rather daunting, however, not to mention impractical if you like to cook with fresh ingredients. What I have found works for me is shopping two or three times a week. The food is fresher (like my parents, I use my freezer mostly for ice cream), and I don't have to try to imagine what I might feel like eating two weeks from now.

There may be times when you may not even need to go shopping. You can open the refrigerator and make dinner from what you already have. Some of my most successful meals have been created this way. To this end, I have included a chapter on basic staples that an Italian kitchen should be stocked with. I have a similar chapter in my first book, *The Classic Pasta Cookbook,* and readers have commented on how easily they have created meals from what they already had in the house.

I am too often asked to make wine suggestions for my recipes. My usual answer is to choose a wine that you like. I know that might sound glib, but I mean it sincerely. Just as preferences for different foods are personal, so is wine a matter of personal taste. When I choose a wine for a meal, I think about the wine I feel like drinking, rather than what goes best with what I will eat. If I am in the mood for a full-bodied red, that is what I will choose, regardless of whether I am having lamb, chicken, or fish. I do not mean to imply that food has no effect on how wine tastes. In fact, when I find a wine I like, I will buy a case and have it all the time for a while. I enjoy how it tastes a little different with each meal. My advice is to identify the characteristics you enjoy most in a wine, then find out which wines are likely to have those characteristics. If you ask your wine merchant what would go well with a certain dish, he or she might tell you what they like, but it may not be what you like. But if you ask them to recommend wines that have qualities you are looking for, you are more likely to end up with a wine you'll like.

Using the right equipment is also very important in making cooking easier. Having a sharp chef's knife is essential to me. A sharp knife is actually safer than a dull one and certainly makes chopping or slicing go much faster. The best knives have forged blades rather than the stamped-out blades of the knives sold in supermarkets. To keep your knife sharp, use a steel to straighten the microscopic dents that chopping and cutting put on the edge of the blade. It is only necessary to grind the blade when it needs to be reshaped and that should only occur every nine to twelve months. By keeping the blade sharp with a steel, you will not need to grind it as often, which will lengthen the life of your knife. I prefer wooden cutting boards to plastic ones. I find it easier to chop on wood because my knife is less likely to slip. Having quality pots and pans also makes cooking much easier. The best ones are heavy and have an aluminum or copper core for heat conduction encased in stainless steel for durability and easy cleaning. When heat is distributed evenly, food is less likely to burn. I own a couple of non-stick pans, but I mostly use them to cook eggs or delicate fish fillets. For everything else, I prefer to use stainless-steel pans, whose browning capabilities I find far more effective.

Many people tell me they don't cook when what they really mean is that they don't prepare elaborate meals. But grilling a steak is cooking too. Selecting a choice piece of meat, grilling it just the right amount of time, and seasoning it perfectly with salt and pepper and maybe some wonderful extra-virgin olive oil is simple cooking at its best. I hope this book will help to make cooking less intimidating, not so much a chore as an enjoyable and richly rewarding part of your daily life.

The Italian Pantry

SOME OF THE MOST INTERESTING and delicious dishes have been created when there was no food in the house. The following is a list of staples an Italian kitchen should always be stocked with, as well as a few specialty items certain recipes call for. In addition, good Italian cooking is completely dependent on the quality of ingredients. When a recipe uses only a few ingredients, the quality of each becomes very important.

OLIVE OIL

Olive oil is an essential ingredient in a large number of Italian dishes. It is not simply a cooking oil. The reason for using olive oil is for its flavor, which is why one should use the best possible extra-virgin olive oil one can get. Premium olive oils are not cheap. However, even a one-liter bottle of olive oil at 30 dollars comes to just 45 cents a tablespoon. One of my favorite ways to eat shrimp is to boil them and season them with olive oil and lemon. Most people would not think twice about spending 10 dollars or more for a pound of good-quality shrimp, so why waste those shrimp on olive oil that doesn't taste wonderful?

Now that you are convinced that you should use a good olive oil comes the hard part—finding one. Although you can be fairly certain that a cheap bottle of oil will not be good, just because an oil is expensive does not guarantee its quality. The only way to find an olive oil that you like is to taste several. A good way to do this is to hold an olive oil party. Each guest brings a different bottle of oil and the host prepares some boiled new potatoes (they provide a perfect neutral vehicle with which to taste olive oil). You will get to taste many different oils and the cost will be no more than a bottle of olive oil and some potatoes!

SALT

Naturally, if you have a medical condition that does not permit the use of salt, you should avoid it. For the rest of us, however, salt is essential in cooking. Used judiciously, salt will bring out the depth and nuance of flavor in a dish that would taste bland without it. When the right amount of salt is used, food should not taste salty. Using spices instead of salt only adds extraneous flavors that often end up masking the taste of the main ingredients. I prefer using sea salt. I find it has a pure flavor with no bitter aftertaste. I use fine rather than coarse because it dissolves more easily in the food.

PEPPER

Use only pepper that you grind as needed from a peppermill. Black pepper's fragrant aroma is a volatile oil that is released when it is ground. With preground pepper, all you get is the heat and none of its fragrance.

CANNED TOMATOES

If wonderful fresh, ripe tomatoes are available, either from your garden or a local farmers' market, by all means use fresh whenever tomatoes are called for. Otherwise, good canned peeled whole tomatoes are usually a better choice than most supermarket fresh tomatoes. The best tomatoes imported from Italy are a variety called San Marzano. They are pear-shaped and come from a small town of the same name near Naples. Unfortunately, not all brands that say San Marzano on the label are good. I have seen cans of tomatoes labeled San Marzano that were not even imported from Italy but were grown domestically using San Marzano tomato seeds. There are so many different brands available that it is best to sample several to determine which brand to buy on a regular basis. Taste a piece of tomato right out of the can. It should have a firm texture and a sweet, ripe flavor without being too salty.

RICE

To make risotto, it is necessary to use a particular kind of rice. Arborio is probably the best-known variety, but there are others that are starting to become available as well. Carnaroli, creamy yet wonderfully chewy, is considered by many to be the prince of risotto rices. Vialone Nano is a short-grain rice that is the favorite of Venetians. All three, however, share a characteristic that is indispensable for making risotto. They are composed of two kinds of starches: a translucent starch on the outside that mostly melts away in the cooking process and is what makes a risotto creamy, and a solid white starchy core that expands as it cooks and causes the rice kernel to swell.

PASTA

All the pasta dishes in this book call for dried flour-and-water store-bought pasta. This is not a compromise. It is the kind of pasta that is best suited to these particular recipes. Egg pasta, which is best when it is homemade, is a more delicate pasta that is much more absorbent and goes well with delicate cream- and butter-based sauces.

A good-quality flour-and-water pasta will have a satisfyingly chewy texture and the subtle flavor of premium-quality golden yellow semolina (durum wheat flour). Premium brands I like include Latini, Martelli, Rustichella, and Giuseppe Cocco. More commonly available brands I like are Barilla and DeCecco.

DRIED PORCINI MUSHROOMS

These dried mushrooms have a rich, intense flavor and are not used only when fresh porcini are unavailable. Dried porcini add richness to risottos, pasta sauces, and stews. They will last forever if wrapped airtight in plastic wrap or Ziploc bags and kept in the refrigerator. Look for packages that have large slices of whole mushrooms; less-expensive brands often are primarily stems.

PARMIGIANO-REGGIANO

Although the term "parmesan" can mean any hard grating cheese, there is only one cheese made in a limited area surrounding Parma (north of Bologna) according to strict guidelines that may be called Parmigiano-Reggiano. It is produced the same way it has been for the past seven hundred years, and although cheese factories have benefited from modern technological advances, the production of a wheel of Parmigiano-Reggiano is still dependent on the skills of the individual cheesemaker that have been passed down from generation to generation. It is a cheese of incomparable flavor, texture, and richness that must age a minimum of eighteen months before it can be sold.

Using it only as a grating cheese would be depriving yourself of the pleasure of eating one of the world's best table cheeses. Serve it with walnuts at the end of a meal while finishing a bottle of Amarone, or place a few drops of balsamic vinegar over small chunks for an extraordinary hors d'oeuvre. When using it grated, do not grate it too far in advance or, even worse, have it grated for you when you buy it. As soon as it is grated, Parmigiano-Reggiano begins to dry out and lose some of its aroma. Ideally you should grate it at the last minute, which is very easy to do with a drum-type grater.

Parmigiano-Reggiano will keep for a long time in the refrigerator, even three to four months, if stored properly. For a piece that is larger than a pound, I recommend cutting it into smaller pieces so that you are not unwrapping and rewrapping the same piece. Wrap each piece in plastic or, even better, in a Ziploc bag, taking care to squeeze out all the air before sealing it. Parmigiano-Reggiano stored for a long time may develop mold on the surface. This is normal. Simply scrape it off with a knife, and the cheese will be fine.

PECORINO ROMANO

Pecorino is any sheep's milk cheese, and pecorino romano usually refers to an aged cheese that is mostly used for grating. It is sharper than Parmigiano-Reggiano, so use it sparingly. A good-quality imported brand will have an intense rich flavor and is good enough to eat on its own. Keep it in the refrigerator wrapped in plastic or sealed in a Ziploc bag.

PANCETTA

Pancetta is basically Italian bacon. It is round because it has been rolled, and if you unravel it, you will see that it looks just like a slice of bacon. There are, however, two important differences between pancetta and bacon. First, pancetta is not smoked (unless you are in Venice or the Alto Adige region of Italy near Austria, where almost all the cured meats are smoked), and second, it is cured. The curing process is similar to that of prosciutto, where the hams are salted, then hung to air-cure for at least twelve months. Pancetta cures in less time because it is smaller but, like prosciutto, at the end of the process is ready to eat as is without needing to be cooked. In Italy you will find pancetta often included on a platter of assorted cold cuts. If you must substitute bacon, you can take away most of the smoky flavor by putting it in boiling water for a couple of minutes.

GARLIC

Garlic is used with a light hand in Italian cooking. Italians in Italy who walk into a restaurant and are instantly greeted by the smell of garlic are likely to turn around and walk back out. Even when a large amount of garlic is called for in a recipe, it is only sautéed briefly, so that the flavor is mild rather than pungent.

I cannot pass up the opportunity to put in my two cents on the great "to remove or not to remove the green shoot" controversy. A green shoot means that the garlic is sprouting and is therefore old. The best thing to do is to buy some fresh garlic. If you discard the green shoot, you are simply throwing away the freshest part!

CAPERS

Capers are the unopened flowers of the caper bush. They are available preserved either in vinegar or in salt. The ones in vinegar are by far the most common; their advantage is that they keep forever. They take on the flavor of the vinegar, however, and no amount of rinsing will remove it. I prefer capers preserved in salt because the salt simply preserves them and brings out their own natural flavor. Keep them in the refrigerator and discard them when you see the salt begin to yellow. Rinsing and soaking them in several changes of water before using them is essential, or they will taste excessively salty.

ANCHOVIES

Even if you have had a traumatic experience as a child biting down on a slice of pizza with a huge anchovy on top and have forsworn anchovies since, it doesn't mean you won't like a dish that is made with anchovies. When used in cooking, they are almost unnoticeable but they add a richness of flavor that is hard to duplicate. When buying anchovies, look for the ones in glass jars. They are usually of better quality, and you can store them in the jar once they are open rather than transferring them from the tin to another container. If you arc an anchovy lover, however, look for whole anchovies packed in salt that are sold in bulk. They require some work in filleting and cleaning, but they are well worth the effort. Store them in a container with enough olive oil to cover. As long as anchovies are completely covered in oil, they should keep for a minimum of several weeks in the refrigerator.

PARSLEY

There is an expression in Italian that describes someone who seems to pop up all the time. We say that he or she is "like parsley" because so many Italian dishes call for parsley. I prefer to use the Italian flat-leaf variety, not out of any patriotic motivation, but because I prefer the flavor. I find curly parsley to be harsher and less aromatic.

HERBS

Using fresh herbs is always preferable to dried, but sometimes one does not have a choice. It seems that if I need sage, when I go to the market there is every herb imaginable except sage. Unless, of course, I am looking for rosemary, in which case that is the only herb missing. This is why I always keep dried herbs on hand. It is important to buy only dried whole leaves. Crumbled, crushed, or powdered herbs have little or no fragrance and are simply pungent. When using dried herbs, always chop them a bit to release their aromas.

WINE

Wine for cooking need not be very expensive or rare vintage, but it should be a wine that you would also enjoy drinking.

Some Essential Techniques

Here are a few tricks of the trade that will make the preparation for the recipes in this book simple and easy. The illustrations will show you techniques such as how to keep your knife sharp and how to chop an onion in less time than it takes for it to make you cry.

PEELING A TOMATO

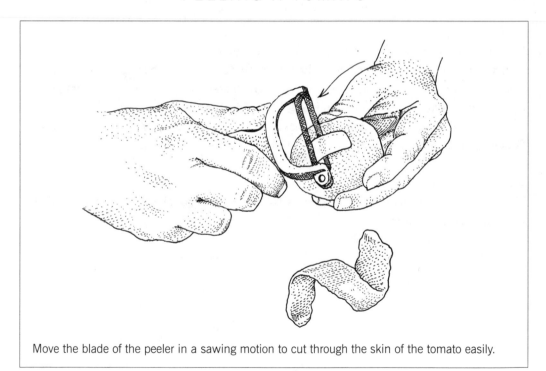

Move the blade of the peeler in a sawing motion to cut through the skin of the tomato easily.

CHOPPING AN ONION

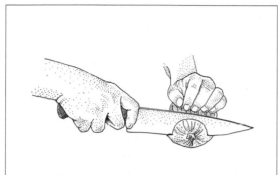

1. Cut off the top of the onion but not the root end.

2. Place the onion with the cut end on the cutting board and cut in half lengthwise. Remove the skin.

3. Place the onion with the flat end down and make lengthwise cuts close together following the round shape of the onion and keeping the root end intact.

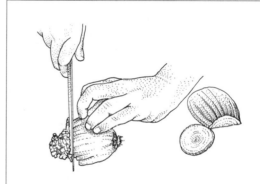

4. Cut the onion in thin slices perpendicular to the cuts made in the previous step to produce finely chopped onion.

CUTTING A PEPPER

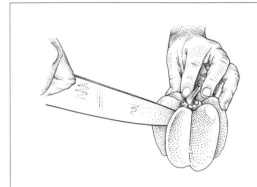

1. Hold the pepper with the top down and cut it open along the grooves using the tip of your knife.

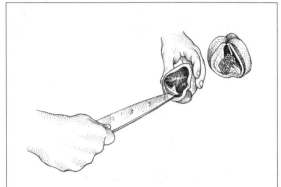

2. Cut away the white pith inside the pepper. Discard the stem, core, and seeds.

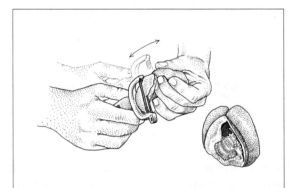

3. Peel the pepper by moving the blade of the peeler in a sawing motion.

HOW TO SHARPEN A KNIFE WITH A STEEL

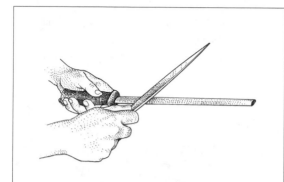

1. Place the handle end of the blade at a slight angle on the steel.

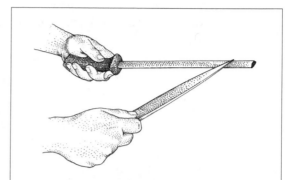

2. Slide the blade along the steel away from you until the tip of the knife reaches the end of the steel.

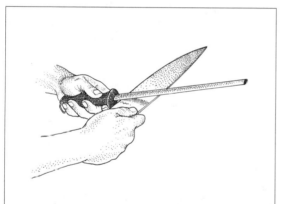

3. Repeat with the other side of the blade.

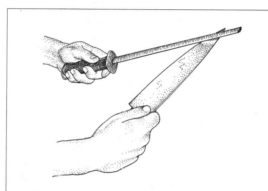

4. Continue alternating sides until both sides of the blade have passed over the steel 5 or 6 times.

TRIMMING ARTICHOKES

This is a way to trim artichokes so that what is left is completely edible. The technique mimics what you do when you eat a whole artichoke leaf by leaf. The part you keep is the part you would scrape with your teeth at the bottom of the leaf. Have a cut lemon on hand so that you can rub any parts you cut to prevent them from turning black. Squeeze another lemon into a bowl of cold water for the finished artichokes.

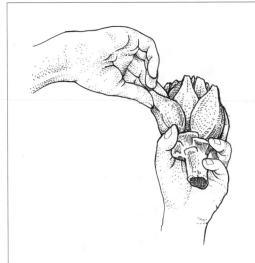

1. Begin by snapping the leaves back and pulling them down to remove them. The tender part at the bottom should stay attached to the artichoke. Continue until you see the lighter tender part come halfway up the leaf.

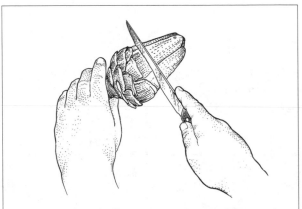

2. Using a sharp knife, cut across the top of the remaining leaves where the tender part ends.

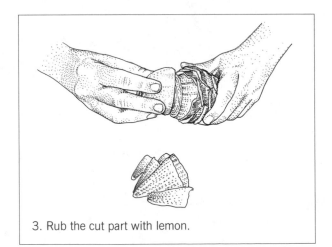

3. Rub the cut part with lemon.

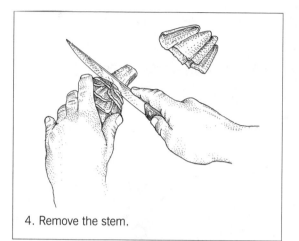

4. Remove the stem.

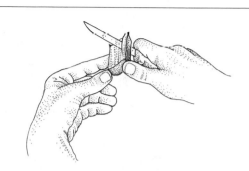

5. Trim it so that only the center core remains. This is the best part of the artichoke and tastes just like the heart. Drop it into the bowl of lemon water.

6. With a paring knife, trim the outside of the artichoke to remove all the dark green parts. Rub with the lemon when done.

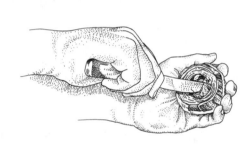

7. Using a dinner knife with a rounded tip, pry the choke out.

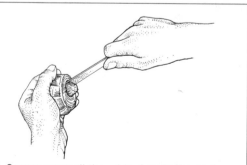

8. Scrape away all the white fuzz in the center.

9. Put the trimmed artichoke into the lemon water until you are ready to cook it.

EASY BONING OF A WHOLE CHICKEN BREAST

2 POUNDS BONE-IN WHOLE CHICKEN BREASTS
WILL YIELD APPROXIMATELY 1½ POUNDS BONELESS, SKINLESS FILLETS

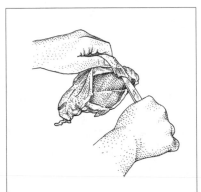

1. Remove the skin beginning at the sides, where the ribs are. Use a paring knife to cut where it is attached.

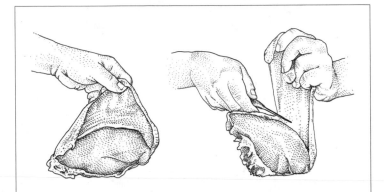

2. Once the skin is attached only at the center of the chicken breast, grab it with one hand, so that it is taut, and cut it away with your knife.

3. At the thick part of the chicken breast you will see the two joints where the wings were attached. Beginning on one side of the breast, slip your finger in the opening that is right next to the joint.

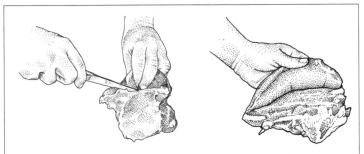

4. With your knife, cut the meat away from the sides, where the ribs were, until the piece of meat is only attached at the center of the breast. Repeat steps 3 and 4 on the other side.

5. Grab the meat just like the skin and cut it away with the knife. Repeat the same procedure on the other side.

6. Now remove the two tenderloins that are still attached to the carcass. All that holds them attached is the membrane that covers them. Using the tip of the paring knife, cut the membrane where it is attached to the bone.

7. Slide your finger under the tenderloin to loosen it.

8. The tenderloin is still attached to the carcass at one end by a white tendon. Grab the tenderloin and gently yank it loose.

9. To remove the white tendon from the two tenderloins, grab the little bit that sticks out with a paper towel so it won't slip. Holding the meat in place with the dull side of your knife, gently pull the tendon out.

FILLETING A CHICKEN BREAST

To keep chicken moist and tender, it needs to cook very quickly. This is best done by cutting the large breast pieces horizontally in half to obtain thin fillets. (Pounding is not good for chicken because it is so delicate that it breaks the fibers and ruins the texture of the meat.)

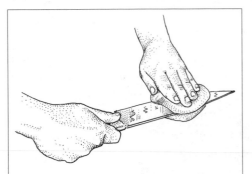

1. Place the piece to be cut on the edge of the cutting board and hold it down with one hand while you cut with the other, starting at the thickest end. If the chicken breast is particularly large, you may cut three fillets out of each piece.

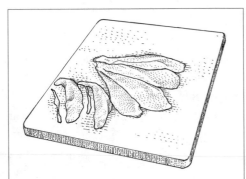

2. Boned chicken breasts (four fillets and two tenderloins).

Appetizers

Fresh Tuna, Arugula, and Tomato

TONNO FRESCO E RUCOLA

This savory concoction is perfect for a summer lunch or as a substantial appetizer. It is just as good when the tuna is still hot from the grill or at room temperature. If you want to assemble everything ahead of time, wait until the last minute to dress it.

25 *minutes from start to finish*

12 ounces fresh tuna, sliced about 1 inch thick
1 tablespoon extra-virgin olive oil, plus more to dress the salad
Salt
Freshly ground black pepper

8 ounces arugula
2 large vine-ripened tomatoes, or 5 or 6 plum tomatoes (about 12 ounces)
4 teaspoons capers
1 tablespoon red wine vinegar
1 tablespoon balsamic vinegar

1. Light the grill.

2. Place the tuna on a platter and drizzle the olive oil over it. Season with salt and pepper and turn the fish until it is well coated.

3. Remove the longer stems from the arugula, rinse the leaves, and spin dry. Place in a serving bowl.

4. Cut the tomatoes in half and scoop out the seeds. Cut them into about ½-inch dice. Add the cut tomatoes to the bowl.

5. When the grill is very hot, put on the tuna. I like it medium-rare and cook it for 3 to 4 minutes on each side. Remove from the grill.

6. Cut the tuna into ¾-inch cubes and add it to the bowl along with the capers. When ready to serve, dress with some salt, enough olive oil to coat the leaves, and both vinegars.

SERVES 6 PEOPLE AS AN APPETIZER OR 4 PEOPLE AS A MAIN DISH

Crostini with Tomatoes and Arugula

CROSTINI AL POMODORO E RUCOLA

This fresh-tasting variation of the now very popular bruschetta comes from the restaurant Trattoria della Nonna in Mattinata on the dramatic coast of the Gargano in Apulia, Italy.

minutes from start to finish **20**

1 pound fresh, ripe plum tomatoes
12 medium-size fresh basil leaves
2 tablespoons fresh oregano leaves
1 medium bunch arugula (about
   3 ounces)

1 medium loaf of Italian bread or a
   French baguette
Salt
3 tablespoons extra-virgin olive oil

1. Preheat the broiler.

2. Peel the tomatoes (page 24), remove the seeds, and cut into ½-inch dice. Place the tomatoes in a mixing bowl.

3. Coarsely chop the basil and oregano leaves and add them to the tomatoes. Trim the arugula stems, rinse and dry the leaves, coarsely shred them, and add them to the bowl.

4. Cut 12 slices of bread on a diagonal about ½ inch thick. Place the slices on a baking sheet and put it under the broiler. (Or place them on a grill, which imparts a very nice flavor.) Broil the bread until it becomes lightly browned, 2 to 3 minutes, then turn the slices over and brown the second side as well.

5. Season the tomato mixture with salt, add the olive oil, and toss well. Spread the tomato mixture over the bread slices and serve.

MAKES 12 CROSTINI

Grilled Mushrooms with Balsamic Vinegar

FUNGHI AI FERRI ALL' ACETO BALSAMICO

A small amount of a very good balsamic vinegar gives these mushrooms a wonderfully rich and intense flavor. They can be served either warm or at room temperature, which makes them perfect for a buffet, an appetizer, or a side dish.

15 *minutes from start to finish*

12 ounces cremini or white mushrooms	Pinch of crushed red pepper flakes
3 tablespoons extra-virgin olive oil	Salt
1 teaspoon balsamic vinegar	Freshly ground black pepper

1. Light the grill. While it is getting hot, wipe any dirt from the mushrooms. Place them in a mixing bowl and toss them with half of the olive oil.

2. When the grill is hot, place the mushrooms on their side on the grill rack. If it is a gas grill, turn the flame down to medium; if using charcoal, set the rack about 3 inches from the fire. Cover the grill and cook for about 5 minutes, turning the mushrooms halfway through. Remove the mushrooms and cut them in half. Put them back in the mixing bowl and add the balsamic vinegar, red pepper flakes, the remaining olive oil, and salt and pepper to taste. Toss well and serve warm or at room temperature.

SERVES 4 TO 6 PEOPLE

Gratinéed Mussels

COZZE IN GRATICOLA

These mussels make tasty finger food before your guests sit down to dinner or for cocktail parties. You can prepare them ahead of time so that when you are ready to serve, all you need to do is run the mussels under the broiler.

minutes from start to finish **25**

1 pound mussels, the larger the better
2 tablespoons finely chopped Italian
    flat-leaf parsley
1½ teaspoons finely chopped garlic

2 tablespoons extra-virgin olive oil
1 tablespoon plain fine dry bread
    crumbs, plus more for topping
Salt

1. Preheat the broiler.

2. Scrub the mussels well and remove any beards. Put them in a large skillet with about ¼ cup water. Cover and place over high heat. After a few minutes, the mussels should begin to open. Remove them from the pan as soon as they open and set aside.

3. Place the parsley and garlic in a mixing bowl with the olive oil and bread crumbs. Mix well.

4. Remove the bodies of the mussels from the shells, keeping half the shells, and add them to the parsley mixture. Season with salt and toss until the mussels are thoroughly coated with the mixture.

5. Place the reserved shells on a baking sheet. Place a mussel in each half-shell, making sure to use all of the parsley mixture. Top with a sprinkling of bread crumbs.

6. Broil the mussels until lightly browned, 5 minutes or less. Serve hot or warm, and eat them with toothpicks.

SERVES 4 TO 6 PEOPLE

Stuffed Squid with Chickpea Sauce

CALAMARI RIPIENI CON SALSA DI CECI

When prepared with care, squid are delicate and very tender. Deep-frying is only one of the many ways squid can be prepared. Italian cooks use them in pasta sauces and risottos, stew them with tomatoes, or fill them with delicious stuffings. I tasted this simple and flavorful appetizer at a seaside restaurant called Teresa in Pesaro on the Adriatic coast, about 140 miles south of Venice. I prefer to eat it hot, although it is also very good at room temperature.

25 *minutes to prepare*

70 *minutes from start to finish*

1 pound cleaned squid tubes and
   tentacles (the sacs should be at least
   2 inches long)
½ teaspoon finely chopped garlic
2 tablespoons finely chopped Italian
   flat-leaf parsley
2 tablespoons freshly grated Parmigiano-
   Reggiano
Salt
Freshly ground black pepper
1 tablespoon red wine vinegar

For the Sauce:
1 cup drained canned chickpeas
4 tablespoons extra-virgin olive oil
2 tablespoons freshly squeezed lemon
   juice
Salt
Freshly ground black pepper

1. Place a pot of water that will comfortably hold the squid over high heat and bring to a boil.

2. Rinse the squid, making sure the sacs are clean. If the heads are still attached to the tentacles, cut off just below the eyes and squeeze out the beak.

3. Put the tentacles in a food processor, chop very fine, and transfer to a mixing bowl. Add the garlic, parsley, and Parmigiano-Reggiano, season with salt and pepper, and mix well. Place the filling in the squid sacs, making sure they are no more than two-thirds full, as they will shrink as they cook. Close the opening of the sacs with toothpicks.

4. Add the vinegar to the boiling water and put in the squid. When the water comes back to a boil, lower the heat to a gentle simmer and cover the pot. Cook until the squid feel very tender when gently pierced with a toothpick, about 45 minutes. Remove the pot from the heat but leave the squid in their poaching liquid so that they do not dry out and become tough.

5. To prepare the sauce, put the chickpeas, olive oil, and lemon juice in a food processor and pulse until creamy. Season with salt and pepper and add ½ cup of the squid poaching liquid. Process until the sauce is smooth and as thick as rich heavy cream.

6. When ready to serve, take the squid out of the poaching water and slice the sacs into rings about ¼ inch thick. (If the squid have cooled down and you wish to serve them hot, simply reheat them gently in their poaching liquid.) Place the squid on a plate and pour the sauce over them.

SERVES 4 TO 6 PEOPLE

Thinly Sliced Sea Bass Marinated in Lemon

BRANZINO MARINATO AL LIMONE

This is a very refreshing and elegant appetizer in which very thin slices of fish are actually cooked by steeping them in a marinade of lemon juice and fresh herbs, as for seviche. The amount of lemon juice called for may seem excessive, but most of the acidity is consumed in this process so that the "cooked" fish slices have only a hint of lemon left.

20 *minutes to prepare*

3 *hours from start to finish*

12 ounces skinless sea bass (not Chilean), striped bass, or grouper fillet

½ cup freshly squeezed lemon juice, plus more if needed

⅓ cup very finely diced red onion

2 tablespoons finely chopped Italian flat-leaf parsley

1 teaspoon chopped fresh marjoram leaves

2 tablespoons extra-virgin olive oil

Salt

Freshly ground black pepper

1. Cut the fish across the grain on a diagonal into very thin slices and place in a shallow bowl.

2. Add the remaining ingredients, seasoning with salt and pepper, and toss gently. Let marinate at room temperature for 2½ to 3 hours, or until the fish is cooked through. Carefully stir the fish about every hour. To see if it is done, cut a small corner from one of the slices. The center should be opaque and no longer translucent. Taste the marinade occasionally to make sure the fish has not consumed all of the acidity from the lemon. If necessary, add more lemon juice 2 tablespoons at a time.

3. You may serve the fish as soon as it is ready or refrigerate it covered for up to 2 days. Let it come to room temperature before serving.

SERVES 4 TO 6 PEOPLE

Italian Open-Faced Omelet with Scallions

FRITTATA ALLE CIPOLLINE

A frittata makes a perfect light meal or picnic dish since it tastes just as good at room temperature as it does hot. I use Montasio in this recipe, a mildly sharp cow's milk cheese from the area around Venice. A cream Havarti or mild Cheddar may be substituted if necessary.

minutes from start to finish **25**

16 scallions
1½ tablespoons butter
1 tablespoon vegetable oil
Salt
Freshly ground black pepper

2 teaspoons finely chopped Italian
　flat-leaf parsley
4 ounces Montasio, cream Havarti, or
　mild Cheddar
8 extra-large eggs

1. Remove the dark green tops of the scallions (approximately the top third) and trim the root ends. Cut the scallions lengthwise in half, then crosswise into ½-inch pieces. Rinse well in a strainer under cold water.

2. Preheat the oven to 400°F.

3. Put 1 tablespoon of the butter and the vegetable oil in an ovenproof 9- or 10-inch skillet, preferably nonstick. Place over medium heat and add the scallions. Season with salt and pepper and sauté until they are tender and have colored lightly.

4. While the scallions are cooking, chop the parsley and grate the cheese. Break the eggs into a mixing bowl and beat until the whites and yolks are well mixed. Add the parsley, cheese, and a little salt and pepper. Lift the scallions out of the skillet with a slotted spoon, leaving as much of the oil in the pan as possible, and stir them into the egg mixture.

5. Put the remaining ½ tablespoon butter in the skillet and return it to medium heat. When the butter is hot, add the egg mixture and cook, without stirring, for about 5 minutes to set the bottom. Transfer the skillet to the oven and continue cooking until the frittata looks firm when the pan is shaken, about 10 minutes. Remove from the oven and slide the frittata onto a plate. Serve hot or at room temperature.

SERVES 4 TO 6 PEOPLE

Soups

Escarole, Bean, and Barley Soup

ZUPPA DI FAGIOLI E SCAROLA

This recipe was inspired by a soup I ate at one of Milan's finest restaurants, Aimo e Nadia. It was made with a dark green cabbage typical of Tuscany and *farro,* an ancient Etruscan grain. My version uses escarole and barley along with two different beans. Although it is a distant cousin of the original, it maintains the style of hearty Tuscan soups, which are the perfect antidote to a cold winter's day.

20 *minutes to prepare*

60 *minutes from start to finish*

½ cup finely chopped yellow onion
3 tablespoons extra-virgin olive oil
12 ounces escarole, to yield about
    5 cups coarsely chopped leaves
1½ teaspoons chopped fresh rosemary
    leaves
Salt

Freshly ground black pepper
½ cup drained canned cannellini beans
½ cup drained canned chickpeas
½ cup pearl barley
5 cups Homemade Meat Broth (recipe
    follows), or 1 large beef bouillon
    cube dissolved in 5 cups water

1. Put the onion and olive oil in a heavy 6-quart soup pot and place it over medium-low heat. Sauté until the onion turns a light caramel color.

2. While the onion is sautéing, rinse the escarole and coarsely chop the leaves.

3. When the onion is ready, raise the heat to medium-high and add the rosemary and escarole. Season lightly with salt and fairly generously with black pepper. Cook, stirring occasionally, until the escarole is wilted and the water it will have released is evaporated, then sauté for 1 to 2 minutes longer.

4. Add the cannellini beans, chickpeas, and barley. Stir well, then add the broth. Cover the pot. When the soup begins to boil, adjust the heat so that it cooks at a steady simmer. Cook until the barley is tender, about 30 minutes. Remove from the heat and serve.

SERVES 4 TO 6 PEOPLE

Homemade Meat Broth

BRODO DI CARNE

A homemade Italian meat broth is a delicate, light broth made with a combination of meats and vegetables that are not baked (as one does when making brown stock) before placing them in water.

Do not discard the meats when the broth is done. Store them in a container with just enough broth to cover so that they will not dry out. The meat is excellent served hot with the sauce from the lamb chop recipe on page 141 or the sauce for poached fish on page 97.

minutes to prepare **10**

hours from start to finish **3 ½**

A combination of beef short ribs, veal breast and ribs, and chicken parts (totaling about 5 pounds)
2 carrots, peeled
2 to 3 celery ribs, rinsed
1 medium yellow onion, peeled

1 fresh, ripe peeled (page 24) tomato or whole peeled canned tomato
1 Italian flat-leaf parsley sprig
1 tablespoon whole black peppercorns
1 teaspoon salt

1. Put all the ingredients in a large stockpot and add enough cold water to cover by 2 inches. Cover the pot and bring to a boil over high heat, then turn the heat down to very low and place the cover slightly askew. Cook at a very gentle simmer for 3 hours or more.

2. When the broth is done, pour it through a strainer. The broth will keep in the refrigerator for only 2 days, so it is best to freeze it if you want to keep it longer. Freeze the broth in ice cube trays, then store the frozen cubes in plastic bags in the freezer. You will have the convenience of frozen broth cubes to use as needed.

MAKES ABOUT 2 QUARTS

Porcini Mushroom Soup

MINESTRA AI FUNGHI PORCINI

This soup would ideally be the result of a wild mushroom–picking expedition to the woods after a good rainfall in late autumn. If a variety of fresh wild mushrooms is not available, however, the following version, using dried porcini mushrooms, makes an elegant and flavorful alternative.

50 *minutes from start to finish*

1 ounce dried porcini mushrooms
1 pound cremini or white mushrooms
¼ cup finely chopped yellow onion
2 tablespoons butter
1 tablespoon vegetable oil
1 teaspoon shredded fresh sage leaves, or ½ teaspoon chopped dried sage leaves

Salt
Freshly ground black pepper
1 tablespoon all-purpose flour
4 cups Homemade meat Broth (page 45), or 1 large beef bouillon cube dissolved in 4 cups water
3 tablespoons heavy cream

1. Soak the dried mushrooms in a bowl with 2 cups water for at least 20 minutes. Lift the mushrooms out and squeeze the excess water back into the bowl. Rinse them under cold running water and coarsely chop. Filter the soaking water through a paper towel or coffee filter and set aside.

2. While the dried mushrooms are soaking, wipe the fresh mushrooms clean with a damp cloth or paper towel, and slice the mushrooms very thin.

3. Put the onion, butter, oil, and sage in a heavy soup pot and place it over medium-low heat. Cook, stirring occasionally, until the onion turns a rich golden color.

4. Add the fresh mushrooms, season with salt and pepper, and raise the heat to medium. Cook until most of the water the mushrooms will have released is evaporated. Add the porcini mushrooms and stir. Sprinkle the flour over the mushrooms through a wire-mesh strainer or sifter and stir well.

5. Add the broth along with the filtered porcini soaking water and raise the heat to high. When the soup begins to boil, turn the heat down to medium-low and cover the pot. Cook at a gentle simmer for about 20 minutes.

6. Remove about half of the soup and purée it in a blender or food processor, then pour it back into the pot and stir well. If the soup seems too thick at this point, add a little hot water.

7. Bring the soup back to a simmer and stir in the cream. Remove from the heat and serve.

SERVES 4 TO 6 PEOPLE

Savoy Cabbage and Sausage Soup

ZUPPA DI VERZA E SALSICCIA

This is a thick, satisfying soup that is perfect for a cold winter's day. The sausage can be easily made at home (recipe follows); otherwise use a plain breakfast sausage. Avoid Italian sausages with fennel seeds, whose flavor would be too strong for this soup.

20 *minutes to prepare*

80 *minutes from start to finish*

3 tablespoons butter

6 tablespoons finely chopped yellow onion

8 ounces pork sausage (see note above), casings removed

6 cups shredded Savoy cabbage (about 1¼ pounds)

Salt

Freshly ground black pepper

7 cups Homemade Meat Broth (page 45), or 1 large beef bouillon cube dissolved in 7 cups water

6 to 8 parsley stems

¾ cup rice for risotto, such as Arborio or Carnaroli

1. Melt the butter in a heavy 6- to 8-quart soup pot over medium heat. Add the onion and sauté until it turns a rich golden color.

2. When the onion is ready, add the sausage, break it up with a wooden spoon, and cook until it begins to brown. Add the cabbage and season with salt and pepper. Cook until it is wilted and tender. Add the broth and parsley stems, cover the pot, and cook for 30 minutes. Add the rice (see Note), cover, and cook until the rice is done, about 20 minutes. Serve hot.

N O T E : Once the rice is cooked in the soup, the soup cannot be reheated, because the rice will overcook and become mushy. Cook the rice in just the amount of soup you will be serving.

SERVES 4 TO 6 PEOPLE

Homemade Pork Sausage

SALSICCIA DI MAIALE

The most common pork sausage used in Italy is mild and not heavily spiced, and it is the kind best suited for the recipes in this book. It is really very simple to make, and unless you need links, no special equipment is needed. You can increase this recipe to make a larger batch and freeze it in portions.

minutes to prepare 5

1 pound ground pork
1 teaspoon salt
1 teaspoon freshly ground black
    pepper

1 teaspoon finely chopped fresh rose-
    mary leaves, or ½ teaspoon dried
½ teaspoon finely chopped garlic
2 tablespoons dry white wine

1. Combine all the ingredients in a bowl and mix thoroughly with your hands.

2. Wrap in plastic wrap and refrigerate overnight to allow the flavors to blend before cooking or freezing.

MAKES I POUND

Classic Tuscan Vegetable Soup

LA RIBOLLITA

Tuscan soups make you feel like a welcome and pampered guest. The slow, lengthy cooking allows the vegetables to impart the richness of flavor for which this soup is famous. The ingredients may vary according to what is available, but beans and *cavolo nero* are always present. *Cavolo nero* is a Tuscan dark green, leafy vegetable that at the time I am writing is difficult to find in the States except at some specialty markets. I have come up with a combination of vegetables that approximates the flavor as closely as possible. The soup is completely vegetarian, since water is used instead of broth, and it will keep in the refrigerator for several days. In fact, this is one of those dishes that improves after a day or two.

30 *minutes to prepare*

2 1/2 *hours from start to finish*

¼ cup finely chopped yellow onion
3 tablespoons extra-virgin olive oil, plus more for serving
1 medium leek
8 ounces Savoy cabbage
8 ounces red cabbage
8 ounces Swiss chard leaves
⅓ cup diced (¼ inch) peeled celery
⅓ cup diced (¼ inch) peeled carrots
¾ cup diced (½ inch) zucchini
1 cup drained canned cranberry or cannellini beans

1 cup canned whole peeled tomatoes with their juice, coarsely chopped
8 ounces white boiling potatoes, peeled and cut into ½-inch dice
Salt
Freshly ground black pepper
1 slice good crusty bread for each serving (optional)
About 1 tablespoon freshly grated Parmigiano-Reggiano for each serving

1. Put the onion and olive oil in a heavy 6- to 8-quart soup pot and place it over medium-low heat. Sauté until the onion turns a light golden color.

2. While the onion is sautéing, trim the leek by cutting away the root end and the tough green tops of the leaves. Cut the leek lengthwise in half, then crosswise into ½-inch pieces. Soak

the leek in cold water to loosen any dirt. When the onion is done, lift the leek out of the water and add to the pot.

3. Add the following vegetables as you prepare them, periodically stirring the contents of the pot.

Savoy cabbage: Cut off the root end and finely shred it.

Red cabbage: Cut out the core and finely shred the leaves.

Swiss chard: Remove the stems. Rinse the leaves in cold water, then very coarsely chop them.

Celery: Peel the stalk to remove any tough strings, then rinse under cold water and dice.

Carrot: Peel and dice.

Zucchini: Scrub under cold water and dice.

Canned beans: Simply drain them of their liquid.

Canned tomatoes: Coarsely chop or simply break them up with your fingers.

Potatoes: Peel and cut into ½-inch dice. Rinse them by placing them in a bowl of cold water as you cut them.

4. When you have finished adding all the vegetables, season them with salt and pepper. Pour in 5 cups of water, cover the pot, and raise the heat. When the soup comes to a boil, turn the heat down so that it cooks at a gentle simmer. Cook for at least 2 hours, checking it about every 30 minutes to make sure it is still simmering gently. The soup is done when the vegetables are very tender, almost creamy.

5. When you are ready to serve the soup, toast or grill the slices of bread, if using, and place each one in the bottom of a soup plate. Ladle the hot soup over the bread and let it stand for about 5 minutes. Just before serving, drizzle a little olive oil over each serving and sprinkle with the Parmigiano-Reggiano cheese.

SERVES 8 TO 10 PEOPLE

Wild Mushroom and Potato Soup

ZUPPA COI FUNGHI E PATATE

On the Italian Riviera, just outside the town of Camogli, there is a wonderful restaurant called Ü Giancú that provides entertainment as well as excellent food. As you wait for your meal, you can pass the time by reading the extraordinary collection of original cartoons that adorns the walls. At the end of the meal, the owner comes around with chilled pear grappa in a glass pitcher with a long narrow spout. He tests your stamina by seeing how much grappa he can pour into your mouth before you beg for mercy. While I still had a clear head and palate, I tasted a delicious soup of fresh porcini and potatoes. In attempting to re-create both the flavor and texture, I came up with the following recipe using a mixture of dried porcini and fresh shiitake mushrooms.

15 *minutes to prepare*

45 *minutes from start to finish*

1 ounce dried porcini mushrooms	1 pound boiling potatoes
¾ cup finely chopped yellow onion	Freshly ground black pepper
4 tablespoons extra-virgin olive oil	3½ cups Homemade Meat Broth (page
12 ounces fresh shiitake mushrooms	45), or 1 large beef bouillon cube
Salt	dissolved in 3½ cups water

1. Put the dried porcini in a bowl with 1½ cups water and soak for about 15 minutes.

2. Put the onion and olive oil in a 6-quart soup pot and place it over medium-low heat. Sauté the onion until it turns a light caramel color.

3. While the onion is sautéing, wipe the shiitake mushrooms clean with a damp paper towel and trim the stems. Slice the mushrooms lengthwise about ⅛ inch thick.

4. When the onions are ready, add the shiitake mushrooms and season lightly with salt. Cook for about 5 minutes, stirring occasionally to prevent the mushrooms from sticking to the bottom of the pot.

5. While the mushrooms are cooking, peel the potatoes and cut into ½-inch cubes. As you work, place the cut potatoes in cold water to prevent them from turning brown.

6. Lift the soaked porcini out of the water and squeeze the excess water back into the bowl. Filter the soaking water through a paper towel or coffee filter and set aside. Briefly rinse the porcini and coarsely chop them.

7. Drain the potatoes and add them to the pot along with the porcini. Season with a little more salt and some black pepper. Stir for about 1 minute, then add the broth and porcini soaking water. Cover and bring to a boil over high heat, then adjust the heat so that the soup simmers steadily. Cook until the potatoes are tender, about 30 minutes. Serve hot.

SERVES 4 TO 6 PEOPLE

Celery Root and Potato Soup
MINESTRA DI PATATE E FONDO DI SEDANO

If you like celery, eating celery root is like having the best part of the celery, the heart. It is wonderful raw, cut into narrow sticks, in a salad or sautéed with carrots, and in this soup with potatoes. The soup is puréed, and although it is good on its own, it is even better with some croutons. You can easily make your own by frying some bread cubes in vegetable oil.

30 *minutes from start to finish*

½ cup finely chopped yellow onion

3 tablespoons extra-virgin olive oil

4 cups diced (½ inch) peeled celery root (about 1¼ pounds)

4 cups diced (½ inch) peeled boiling potatoes (about 1½ pounds)

Salt

Freshly ground black pepper

4 cups Homemade Meat Broth (page 45), or 1 large beef bouillon cube dissolved in 4 cups water

Croutons (optional)

1. Put the onion and olive oil in a heavy 6-quart soup pot and place it over medium-low heat. Sauté the onion until it turns a light caramel color.

2. While the onion is sautéing, peel and dice the celery root and potatoes. Once the onion has colored, add the celery root and potatoes and season with salt and pepper. Add the broth. Cover the pot and bring to a boil, then adjust the heat so the soup simmers. Cook until the vegetables are tender, about 15 minutes.

3. Using a slotted spoon, lift out the potatoes and celery root and purée them in a food mill or food processor. Stir the puréed vegetables back into the soup and serve hot, with croutons if desired.

SERVES 4 TO 6 PEOPLE

Rustic Soup with Chickpeas and Porcini

ZUPPA CAMPAGNOLA

Dried porcini mushrooms give this chickpea soup a rich woodsy flavor. I like to mash some of the chickpeas to give it a thicker consistency.

minutes to prepare **15-20**
minutes from start to finish **60**

1 ounce dried porcini mushrooms
⅓ cup diced (¼ inch) peeled carrots
⅓ cup diced (¼ inch) celery
3 to 4 garlic cloves, lightly crushed and
    peeled
3 tablespoons extra-virgin olive oil
2 teaspoons coarsely chopped fresh sage
    leaves
8 ounces white mushrooms, cut into
    ¼-inch dice

1 small head romaine lettuce,
    shredded (about 4 cups)
2 cups drained canned chickpeas
3 cups Homemade Meat Broth (page
    45), or 1 small beef bouillon cube
    dissolved in 3 cups water
Salt
Freshly ground black pepper

1. Put the dried porcini in a bowl with 1½ cups water. Soak until the mushrooms have softened, 10 to 15 minutes.

2. Put the carrots, celery, garlic, and olive oil in a heavy soup pot and place it over medium-high heat. Sauté until the vegetables begin to color and the garlic is lightly browned. Remove the garlic cloves and stir in the sage.

3. Lift the porcini out of the water and squeeze the excess water back into the bowl. Filter the soaking water through a paper towel or coffee filter and set aside. Coarsely chop the porcini and add them to the pot along with the white mushrooms and romaine. Add about 1⅓ cups of the chickpeas, the broth, and the porcini soaking water. Cover and cook at a steady simmer for about 30 minutes. Mash the remaining ⅔ cup chickpeas and add to the soup. Cook for another 10 minutes. Season with salt and pepper and serve.

SERVES 4 TO 6 PEOPLE

"Wedded" Soup

MINESTRA MARITATA

On my way to Rome from Puglia, I stopped for lunch in the tiny town of Vallesaccarda where I had been told there was a wonderful trattoria called Oasis. I walked into a large, bustling restaurant with a seating capacity that probably exceeded the population of the town. Servers passed from table to table with a seemingly endless procession of large serving platters filled with some of the best simple, home-style food I've eaten. Your plate and your carafe of local wine continued to be refilled until you told them to stop. One of the courses was this soup that, the waiter explained to me, was called a "wedded" soup because it is served with dried cornmeal croutons that supposedly create a perfect union with the soup. To me it was not a match made in heaven, but a slice of grilled or toasted crusty bread, I think, accompanies it nicely instead. The soup itself, however, made with its humble ingredients of cabbage, celery, escarole, and just a few pieces of meat is extraordinary.

20 *minutes to prepare*

80 *minutes from start to finish*

12 ounces Savoy cabbage
12 ounces escarole
1 cup diced (½ inch) celery
3 tablespoons extra-virgin olive oil
1 teaspoon finely chopped garlic
Salt
⅛ teaspoon crushed red pepper flakes
6 cups Homemade Meat Broth (page 45),
    or 1 large beef bouillon cube
    dissolved in 6 cups water

Leaves of 4 or 5 Italian flat-leaf parsley
    sprigs
6 ounces beef chuck, cut into ¾-inch
    cubes
1 thick (¾ inch) slice good crusty bread
    for each serving (optional)

1. Cut a slice off the bottom of the Savoy cabbage where it is brown, discard any wilted leaves, and finely shred it. Trim the escarole in the same manner and coarsely chop it. Peel and cut the celery.

2. Put the olive oil and garlic in a heavy 4- to 6-quart soup pot and place it over medium-high heat. When the garlic begins to sizzle and you see that it is about to color, add the vegetables. Season with salt and add the crushed red pepper flakes. Sauté until the cabbage and escarole have wilted, 3 to 4 minutes.

3. Add the broth and turn the heat up to high. When the soup begins to boil, add the parsley leaves and meat. Turn the heat down so that the soup is cooking at a gentle simmer, cover the pot, and cook for about 1 hour.

4. If serving the soup with the bread, toast or grill the slices, place one in the bottom of each soup plate, and ladle the hot soup over it.

SERVES 4 TO 6 PEOPLE

Mini Meatballs in Broth

POLPETTINE IN BRODO

Tiny savory meatballs in broth make a wonderfully simple and comforting soup. Although using a good homemade meat broth is strongly recommended here, in a pinch a good-quality bouillon cube can be used instead.

30 *minutes from start to finish*

5 cups Homemade Meat Broth (page 45), or 1 large beef bouillon cube dissolved in 5 cups water
1 thick slice white bread
2 tablespoons whole milk
8 ounces ground veal
4 ounces ground pork

1 large egg
1¼ cups freshly grated Parmigiano-Reggiano
Pinch of freshly grated nutmeg
Salt
Freshly ground black pepper

1. Place the broth in a soup pot, cover, and bring to a boil over medium-high heat.

2. While the broth is heating, prepare the meatballs. Remove the crust from the bread and soak the bread in the milk until all the milk has been absorbed. Place the ground meats in a mixing bowl. Add the milk-soaked bread, the egg, ¾ cup of the cheese, and the nutmeg. Season with about ½ teaspoon salt and three or four turns of the peppermill. Mix the ingredients together thoroughly with your hands. Roll the mixture into small teaspoon-size meatballs. This is the only part of the recipe that is time-consuming; if you have children, it is an ideal project for them.

3. When you have formed all the meatballs and the broth is boiling, carefully slide the meatballs into the broth and boil for 10 minutes. Ladle the meatballs and broth into soup plates and sprinkle the remaining ½ cup Parmigiano-Reggiano on top. Serve at once.

SERVES 4 TO 6 PEOPLE

Soup in a Bag

MINESTRA NEL SACCHETTO

This soup is not just a conversation piece but also a very good, comforting, easy soup to make. The "bag" is actually cheesecloth in which a dough of flour, eggs, and Parmigiano-Reggiano cheese cooks. Once the dough is cooked, it is taken out of the cloth, diced, and returned to the broth. A well-made homemade meat broth is recommended here, but the soup is also good with a bouillon cube. As the dough cooks, it imparts a wonderful flavor to the broth.

minutes to prepare 30
minutes from start to finish 60

5 cups Homemade Meat Broth (page 45), or 1 large beef bouillon cube dissolved in 5 cups water
3½ tablespoons butter
⅔ cup all-purpose flour

2 large eggs
½ cup freshly grated Parmigiano-Reggiano, plus more (optional) for serving
Pinch of freshly grated nutmeg

1. Put the broth in a soup pot, cover, and bring to a boil over high heat.

2. Melt the butter and pour it into a mixing bowl. Add the flour, eggs, cheese, and nutmeg. Work the mixture with your hands until you obtain a smooth, homogeneous dough.

3. Flatten the dough with your hands into a ½-inch-thick rectangle and wrap it flat in a double layer of cheesecloth. Slip it into the boiling broth, lower the heat, and simmer covered for 20 minutes. Remove the pot from the heat and lift out the dough, which will have become firm. When the dough is cool enough to handle, remove it from the cheesecloth and cut it into ¼-inch cubes.

4. When you are ready to serve, bring the broth back to a boil and put in the cubes of dough. Simmer for about 5 minutes. Serve with some additional Parmigiano-Reggiano if desired.

SERVES 4 TO 6 PEOPLE

Tomato Soup

ZUPPA DI POMODORO

Although I had never been a fan of tomato soup, this recipe opened my eyes (and taste buds) to how fragrant, delicate, and delicious tomato soup can be. The large amount of onions gives this soup richness, and the use of flavorful fresh tomatoes ensures its brightness.

15 *minutes to prepare*

90 *minutes from start to finish*

3 cups yellow onion, halved and very thinly sliced crosswise

4 tablespoons unsalted butter

Salt

1¼ pounds fresh, ripe tomatoes

4 cups Homemade Meat Broth (page 45), or ½ large beef bouillon cube dissolved in 4 cups water

Freshly ground black pepper

Croutons (optional)

1. Put the onion and butter in a heavy 4- to 6-quart soup pot. Place it over medium heat and season lightly with salt to help the onion sweat. Cook until the onion has wilted completely and begins turning a light golden color.

2. While the onion is sautéing, peel the tomatoes (page 24) and coarsely chop them. They should yield approximately 3 cups.

3. When the onion is ready, add the tomatoes and broth. This will make a fairly thin soup that benefits from the addition of croutons. If you prefer a thicker soup, reduce the broth to 3½ cups. Season with salt and pepper and cook covered for about 1 hour at a steady but gentle simmer.

4. When the soup has finished cooking, purée it in the pot using an immersion blender, or in batches in a blender. Taste for salt and pepper. Serve hot, with croutons if you wish.

SERVES 4 TO 6 PEOPLE

Clam Soup with Fresh Tomatoes

ZUPPA DI VONGOLE

When I find very fresh small clams that promise to be tender and tasty (the smaller they are, the more tender they will be), I get an irresistible urge to eat a big bowl of them cooked with nothing but good olive oil, a little garlic, parsley, and some fresh, ripe tomatoes. The broth from this "soup" comes from the juice the clams release as they open. I prefer to eat this without any silverware, using the clam shells as spoons and good crusty bread to soak up the remaining juices.

minutes from start to finish **25**

2 pounds fresh, ripe plum tomatoes

4 tablespoons extra-virgin olive oil

2 teaspoons finely chopped garlic

Pinch of crushed red pepper flakes, or to taste

¼ cup finely chopped Italian flat-leaf parsley

3 tablespoons dry white wine

Salt

4 pounds fresh small clams, thoroughly scrubbed in cold water

1 slice good crusty bread, toasted, for each serving

1. Peel the tomatoes (page 24), scoop out the seeds, and cut into ¼- to ½-inch dice.

2. Put the olive oil and garlic in a sauté pan large enough to accommodate all the clams. Cook over high heat until the garlic is sizzling and you can smell its aroma. Add the red pepper flakes and parsley and stir for about 30 seconds. Add the white wine and allow it to bubble for 1 to 2 minutes so that the alcohol evaporates. Add the tomatoes, season with salt, and cook for about 5 minutes.

3. Add the clams, cover the pan, and cook until all the clams open. You may end up with 2 or 3 stubborn clams that do not open; these are the freshest ones, so resist the temptation to throw them out. Do not leave the pan on the heat, however, or the rest of the clams will become tough. Usually the ones that are still closed can be pried open with your fingers. Serve the soup hot along with the toasted bread.

SERVES 6 TO 8 PEOPLE AS A FIRST COURSE OR 4 PEOPLE AS A MAIN DISH

Pasta and Rice

Spaghetti with Tomatoes and Onions
SPAGHETTI AL POMODORO E CIPOLLE

This is a variation of my mother's famous tomato sauce in which tomatoes are cooked simply with butter and half a peeled onion. I've thinly sliced the onion and sautéed it before adding the tomatoes, which intensifies the sweet flavor of the onion. Either way, there are few dishes that provide as much satisfaction for so little effort. If you are making this at the height of tomato season when you can get wonderful local tomatoes that have real flavor, the extra effort to peel them is well worth it, and you can probably do it in the time it takes the onion to sauté. At other times, good canned whole tomatoes will also deliver excellent results.

35 *minutes from start to finish*

1 cup yellow onion, halved and very thinly sliced crosswise

4 tablespoons unsalted butter

3 cups canned whole peeled tomatoes with their juice, coarsely chopped, or 3 pounds fresh, ripe, flavorful tomatoes, peeled (page 24), seeded, and cut into ½-inch dice

Salt

1 pound spaghetti

⅓ cup freshly grated Parmigiano-Reggiano

Freshly ground black pepper

1. Put the onion and butter in an 8- to 10-inch sauté pan and place it over medium-low heat. Sauté the onion very slowly until it wilts and turns a light caramel color, 10 to 12 minutes.

2. Add the tomatoes and season with salt. Raise the heat a little so that the tomatoes cook at a moderate simmer. Cook the tomatoes until they are no longer watery and you can see the butter separate from the sauce, about 20 minutes.

3. While the tomatoes are cooking, fill a pot for the pasta with at least 4 quarts water and bring to a boil over high heat. When the tomatoes look as if they are almost ready, add 1 tablespoon salt to the water and put in the spaghetti, making sure all the strands are submerged. Cook the pasta until it is al dente. Drain the spaghetti and toss with the sauce. Mix in the grated cheese and season with black pepper. Serve at once.

SERVES 4 TO 6 PEOPLE

Spaghetti with Tomatoes and Anchovies

SPAGHETTI AL POMODORO E ACCIUGHE

This is one of the many recipes in Italian cooking where anchovies add depth of flavor without tasting fishy. The bread crumbs may seem like an unusual ingredient, but they are essential in adding substance to the sauce and helping it cling to the pasta.

minutes from start to finish 30

5 or 6 anchovy fillets
4 tablespoons extra-virgin olive oil
⅓ cup finely chopped yellow onion
2 cups canned whole peeled
    tomatoes with their juice,
    coarsely chopped

Salt
1 pound spaghetti
⅓ cup plain fine dry bread crumbs

1. Coarsely chop the anchovies. Put them in a 10-inch sauté pan with the olive oil and cook over medium-low heat until the anchovies begin to dissolve. Add the onion and sauté until it turns a light caramel color.

2. Meanwhile, fill a pot for the pasta with at least 4 quarts water and place it over high heat.

3. When the onion is ready, add the tomatoes and season lightly with salt (bear in mind that the anchovies are rather salty). Cook until the tomatoes have reduced and there is no more liquid in the pan. Remove from the heat and set aside.

4. Add 1 tablespoon salt to the boiling water and put in the pasta, stirring until all the strands are submerged. Cook the pasta until it is al dente. Drain it and toss with the sauce and bread crumbs. Serve at once.

SERVES 4 TO 6 PEOPLE

Thin Spaghetti with Eggplant, Fresh Tomatoes, and Mozzarella

SPAGHETTINI ALLE MELANZANE E MOZZARELLA

It is hard to go wrong when you put eggplant, tomatoes, and cheese together. Fried eggplant does not have to be heavy and oily. When properly fried over high heat, it will absorb very little oil. The trick is to fry only a few slices at a time and not be afraid to use plenty of oil. Ironically, the less oil you use, the more the eggplant will soak it up.

35 *minutes from start to finish*

1½ pounds fresh, ripe plum tomatoes	1 pound eggplant
1 teaspoon finely chopped garlic	1 pound spaghettini
2 tablespoons extra-virgin olive oil	6 ounces fresh whole-milk mozzarella
Salt	2 tablespoons freshly grated pecorino
Vegetable oil for frying	romano

1. Fill a pot for the pasta with at least 4 quarts water and place it over high heat.

2. Peel the tomatoes (page 24), remove the seeds, and cut them into ½-inch dice.

3. Put the garlic and olive oil in a 10-inch sauté pan and place it over medium-high heat. When the garlic just begins to turn color, add the tomatoes, season with salt, and cook until the tomatoes are no longer watery, 10 to 15 minutes. Remove the pan from the heat.

4. While the tomatoes are cooking, pour at least ¼ inch vegetable oil into a frying pan and place it over high heat. Peel the eggplant and slice it lengthwise about ½ inch thick. When the oil in the pan is hot enough to make the eggplant sizzle, carefully slide in a few of the eggplant slices. Sauté until the bottom has lightly browned, then turn the slices over and brown the other side. Remove the slices, holding them over the pan until the oil stops dripping, and place them on paper towels on a plate. Repeat until all the eggplant is done.

5. Add 1 tablespoon salt to the boiling water and put in the pasta, stirring until all the strands are submerged. Cook the pasta until it is al dente.

6. Meanwhile, cut the fried eggplant into strips about 1½ inches long and ½ inch wide and add them to the tomatoes. Cook for a few minutes over medium-low heat.

7. Cut the fresh mozzarella into small dice.

8. When the pasta is al dente, drain it well and toss with the sauce, adding the mozzarella and pecorino. Serve at once.

SERVES 4 TO 6 PEOPLE

Spaghetti alla Carbonara with Zucchini

SPAGHETTI ALLA CARBONARA CON ZUCCHINE

Diced zucchini provide a surprisingly delicious variation of this classic Roman pasta sauce. Their sweetness mellows the normally robust flavor of this dish. As in the original, the raw eggs are cooked only by tossing with the hot pasta. Use very fresh eggs, or do not do this at all if you are concerned about eating raw eggs. In this version, as well as in the original, I like to use only the yolks, which makes a thicker, richer sauce.

20 *minutes from start to finish*

8 ounces small zucchini
2 tablespoons butter
2 tablespoons extra-virgin olive oil
4 ounces pancetta, sliced ¼ inch thick, cut into strips 1 inch long and ⅛ inch thick
⅓ cup dry white wine
Salt
1 pound spaghetti

4 large egg yolks
3 tablespoons freshly grated Parmigiano-Reggiano
1 tablespoon freshly grated pecorino romano
1 tablespoon finely chopped Italian flat-leaf parsley
Freshly ground black pepper

1. Fill a pot for the pasta with at least 4 quarts water and place it over high heat.

2. Rinse the zucchini (soaking them in cold water will help loosen the dirt if they feel very gritty) and cut into ½-inch dice.

3. Heat the butter and olive oil in a small sauté pan over medium-high heat until the butter is melted. Add the pancetta and cook until it is nicely browned but not crisp. Add the zucchini and continue sautéing until it is tender and lightly browned. Add the white wine and continue cooking until it is reduced by half. Remove from the heat and set aside.

4. When the pasta water has come to a boil, add 1 tablespoon salt and the pasta, stirring until all the strands are submerged.

5. In a large serving bowl, lightly beat the egg yolks with both cheeses, the parsley, a pinch of salt, and several grindings of the peppermill.

6. When the pasta is al dente, set the pan with the pancetta and zucchini over high heat. Drain the pasta and immediately add it to the egg mixture. Toss until it is thoroughly mixed, then add the pancetta and zucchini and toss again. Serve at once.

SERVES 4 TO 6 PEOPLE

Fusilli with Cauliflower
and Black Olives

FUSILLI AL CAVOLFIORE E OLIVE

It is difficult to sauce pasta with cauliflower because it has such a delicate taste and a sauce is supposed to season the pasta. Sautéing the cauliflower long enough, however, intensifies its flavor, and adding olives provides the ideal savory counterpoint, making this a tasty and delicious sauce.

40 *minutes from start to finish*

1 pound cauliflower	⅛ teaspoon crushed red pepper flakes
2 teaspoons finely chopped garlic	Salt
2 tablespoons finely chopped Italian flat-leaf parsley	8 black Greek olives
1½ pounds fresh, ripe plum tomatoes	1 pound fusilli
4 tablespoons extra-virgin olive oil	3 tablespoons freshly grated pecorino romano

1. Bring a pot of water large enough to hold the cauliflower to a boil. Trim the leaves and stem from the cauliflower and add the cauliflower to the boiling water. (White vegetables will taste sweeter if you do not add salt to the boiling water.) Boil the cauliflower until it is tender, 10 to 15 minutes. Drain and cut into pieces no larger than ½ inch.

2. While the cauliflower is cooking, chop the garlic and parsley. Peel the tomatoes (page 24), remove the seeds, and cut into ½-inch dice.

3. Fill a pot for the pasta with at least 4 quarts water and place it over high heat.

4. Put the garlic and olive oil in a 10-inch sauté pan and place it over medium-high heat. Sauté until the garlic begins to sizzle. Add the parsley and red pepper flakes and stir a few times. Add the cauliflower and season with salt. Sauté, stirring occasionally, until the cauliflower is quite tender and begins to brown, 8 to 10 minutes.

5. While the cauliflower is sautéing, cut the olive flesh from the pits and coarsely chop it.

6. When the cauliflower is done, add the tomatoes and cook for 8 to 10 minutes, stirring occasionally.

7. Meanwhile, once you've added the tomatoes to the cauliflower, add 1 tablespoon salt and the fusilli to the boiling pasta water.

8. Just before the pasta is done, add the olives to the sauce, stir well, and remove from the heat. When the pasta is cooked, drain it and toss with the sauce and the grated pecorino cheese. Serve at once.

SERVES 4 TO 6 PEOPLE

Fusilli with Sausage and Leeks

FUSILLI AI PORRI E SALSICCIA

The sweetness of leeks and the savoriness of pork sausage make a wonderful combination in this pasta dish. The sauce is equally good with the long telephone-cord-shaped fusilli or the short spiral fusilli.

35 *minutes from start to finish*

3 medium leeks

8 ounces mild Italian sausage, casings removed, or Homemade Pork Sausage (page 49)

2 tablespoons butter

Salt

Freshly ground black pepper

1 pound fusilli

⅓ cup freshly grated Parmigiano-Reggiano

1. Cut off the root ends of the leeks and trim the tough green tops of the leaves. Cut the leeks crosswise in half and then lengthwise in half again. Cut each quarter in long, very thin strips and place in a large bowl of cold water to soak.

2. Put the sausage and ¼ cup water in a 10- to 12-inch sauté pan and place it over medium-high heat. Break up the sausage with a wooden spoon and cook until all the water is evaporated and the sausage begins to brown lightly.

3. Fill a pot for the pasta with at least 4 quarts water and place it over high heat.

5. Lift the leeks out of the water, so that any dirt remains in the bottom of the bowl. Discard any fat the sausage may have released, add the butter and leeks to the sauté pan, and season with salt and pepper (bear in mind that the sausage is already seasoned). Turn the heat down to medium-low and cover the pan. Cook, stirring occasionally, until the leeks are wilted and very tender, 15 to 20 minutes.

5. After the leeks have been cooking for about 12 minutes and the water for the pasta has come to a boil, add 1 tablespoon salt to the boiling water, put in the pasta, and stir well.

6. While the pasta and the leeks are cooking, grate the cheese.

7. When the leeks are tender, uncover the pan and raise the heat to medium-high. Cook, stirring, until all the water the leeks release evaporates. Remove from the heat.

8. When the pasta is al dente, drain it and toss it with the sauce and grated cheese. Serve at once.

SERVES 4 TO 6 PEOPLE

Bucatini with Sausage and Onions

BUCATINI CON SALSICCIA E CIPOLLA

Savory sausage and sweet onions complement each other perfectly in this simple pasta sauce.

30 *minutes from start to finish*

3 tablespoons butter
2 cups yellow onion, thinly sliced
  lengthwise
1½ pounds fresh, ripe tomatoes
8 ounces Homemade Pork Sausage
  (page 49), or plain pork sausage,
  casings removed

Salt
Freshly ground black pepper
1 pound bucatini
12 to 15 fresh basil leaves
⅓ cup freshly grated Parmigiano-
  Reggiano

1. Put the butter and onion in a 10- to 12-inch skillet or sauté pan and place it over medium-low heat. Sauté until the onion turns a light caramel color.

2. While the onion is sautéing, peel the tomatoes (page 24) and coarsely chop them.

3. When the onion is done, add the sausage to the pan, crumbling it with your fingers. Raise the heat to medium-high and cook the sausage until it has lost its raw color and begins to brown lightly.

4. Fill a pot for the pasta with at least 4 quarts water and place it over high heat.

5. Add the tomatoes to the sausage and season lightly with salt and pepper. Cook until the tomatoes are reduced and all their liquid is evaporated.

6. When the water for the pasta is boiling, add 1 tablespoon salt and put in the pasta, stirring until it is completely submerged.

7. Coarsely chop the basil and add it to the sauce. Cook, stirring, for 1 to 2 minutes and remove from the heat.

8. When the pasta is al dente, drain it and toss it with the sauce and add the Parmigiano-Reggiano. Serve at once.

SERVES 4 TO 6 PEOPLE

Orecchiette with Fresh Tomato, Basil, and Ricotta Salata

ORECCHIETTE AL POMODORO E RICOTTA SALATA

Ricotta salata, also called hard ricotta, together with fresh tomatoes and basil is a much-loved sauce for pasta in Apulia, the region of Italy that extends from the spur of the boot down to the heel. Ricotta salata is fresh ricotta that is aged and hardens to form a wheel of cheese. It retains the creaminess of the fresh cheese but gains a mild pungency from the aging process. Orecchiette, meaning small ears in Italian, are a specialty of the region, and their shape resembles a small ear. In Bari, the capital of Apulia, women make and sell them on the street.

minutes from start to finish **35**

3 pounds fresh, ripe plum tomatoes
⅓ cup finely chopped yellow onion
3 tablespoons extra-virgin olive oil
¼ cup fresh basil leaves

Salt
1 pound orecchiette (see Note)
3 ounces ricotta salata

1. Peel the tomatoes (page 24), remove the seeds, and cut into ½-inch dice.

2. Fill a pot for the pasta with at least 4 quarts water and place it over high heat.

3. Put the onion and olive oil in a 10- to 12-inch sauté pan and place it over medium-low heat. Sauté until the onion turns a rich golden color. Add the tomatoes and raise the heat to medium-high. Chop or tear the basil into small pieces and add to the tomatoes. Season with salt and cook until the tomatoes are reduced and no longer watery, 15 to 20 minutes.

4. When the tomatoes are almost done, add 1 tablespoon salt to the boiling pasta water and put in the pasta. While the pasta is cooking, use a vegetable peeler to shave the ricotta salata into very thin slices (it's okay if it crumbles). (See Note.) When the pasta is al dente, drain it well and toss it with the sauce. Top it with the cheese shavings and serve at once.

N O T E : Suitable alternatives for orecchiette are bucatini (sometimes called perciatelli) and penne. I prefer to sprinkle the cheese on top, but some people like to toss it in with the sauce.

SERVES 4 TO 6 PEOPLE

Bucatini with Broccoli and Sardines, Sicilian Style

BUCATINI COI BROCCOLI E LE SARDE

Using the water the broccoli florets have cooked in to boil the pasta is a little trick that enhances the flavor of this dish.

40 *minutes from start to finish*

⅓ cup golden raisins
Salt
1 pound broccoli florets
½ cup finely chopped onion
4 tablespoons extra-virgin olive oil
4 canned sardines

¼ cup pine nuts
1 pound bucatini
2 tablespoons butter
¼ cup freshly grated Parmigiano-
    Reggiano

1. Put the raisins in a small bowl and cover with water. Set aside.

2. Fill a pot for the pasta with at least 4 quarts water and bring to a boil over high heat. Add 1 tablespoon salt and put in the broccoli florets. Cook until they are quite tender, 6 to 8 minutes.

3. While the broccoli is cooking, put the onion and olive oil in a skillet large enough to accommodate the broccoli and place it over medium heat. Sauté the onion until it turns a light caramel color.

4. Add the sardines to the skillet and break them up with a wooden spoon. Sauté for about 1 minute. Lift the raisins out of the water, squeeze them gently, and add them to the skillet along with the pine nuts. Cook, stirring, for another minute.

5. When the broccoli is cooked, lift it out of the water with a slotted spoon. Put the pasta in the water, stirring until it is completely submerged.

6. Add the broccoli to the skillet and raise the heat to medium-high. Sauté the broccoli with the other ingredients, stirring occasionally. If the broccoli begins to stick to the bottom of

the pan, ladle in a little of the pasta water. Do not worry about the broccoli becoming over-done. The florets should break up while they sauté and will be softer than if you were serving them as a vegetable, because they are meant to be a sauce for pasta and the extra cooking intensifies their flavor.

7. When the pasta is al dente, drain it and toss with the sauce, butter, and Parmigiano-Reggiano. Serve at once.

SERVES 4 TO 6 PEOPLE

Linguine with Shrimp
LINGUINE AI GAMBERI

In Margherita di Savoia, a small town in Apulia just south of the spur of the boot, I feasted on a luscious dish of linguine with fresh *scampi* (a crustacean similar to crayfish). I asked the waiter if he could find out how the sauce was prepared. His response, though not unusual for a restaurant in Italy, is one that I rarely encounter in the States. "There is no need for me to find out. I made it myself!" As of this writing I have not yet found *scampi* in markets here, so in this recipe I have substituted shrimp.

30 *minutes from start to finish*

2 pounds fresh, ripe plum tomatoes
2 teaspoons finely chopped garlic
2 tablespoons extra-virgin olive oil
Small pinch of crushed red pepper flakes
1 pound medium shrimp
    (31 to 40 per pound)

Salt
1 pound linguine
½ cup heavy cream

1. Fill a pot for the pasta with at least 4 quarts water and place it over high heat.

2. Peel the tomatoes (page 24), remove the seeds, and cut into ½-inch dice.

3. Chop the garlic and put it in a 10- to 12-inch skillet or sauté pan with the olive oil. Place the skillet over medium-high heat and sauté until the garlic begins to sizzle (the garlic flavor should be very mild, so do not let it color). Add the tomatoes and red pepper flakes. Cook until most of the water the tomatoes release evaporates. Remove from the heat.

4. While the tomatoes are cooking, peel the shrimp, devein them if necessary, and cut them into pieces about ½ inch long.

5. When the tomatoes are done and the water for the pasta has come to a boil, add 1 tablespoon salt to the water and put in the pasta, stirring until all the strands are submerged.

6. Meanwhile, return the skillet with the tomatoes to medium-high heat, add the cream, and cook until it is reduced by about half. Add the shrimp, season with salt, and cook until they turn pink, 2 to 3 minutes. Remove from the heat.

7. When the pasta is al dente, drain it well, toss it with the sauce, and serve at once.

SERVES 4 TO 6 PEOPLE

Butternut Squash Risotto
RISOTTO AL PROFUMO DI ZUCCA

One of the many glorious dishes available in Venice in the fall is a risotto made with a local pumpkin called *zucca barucca*. Its aroma is rich and sweet, and its deep golden color resembles the changing leaves in the countryside. In the States I have found that butternut squash most closely resembles the flavor of this pumpkin. Risotto is very easy to make. Its most trying requirement is stirring it constantly for the 20 minutes it takes to cook, but you can enlist the assistance of guests or family members to share stirring duty.

45 *minutes from start to finish*

½ cup finely chopped yellow onion
3 tablespoons butter
1 pound butternut squash (about
    3 cups diced)
Salt
Freshly ground black pepper
5 cups Homemade Meat Broth (page 45),
    or 1 large beef bouillon cube
    dissolved in 5 cups water

1½ cups rice for risotto, such as Arborio
    or Carnaroli
2 tablespoons finely chopped Italian
    flat-leaf parsley
½ cup freshly grated Parmigiano-
    Reggiano

1. Put the onion and 2 tablespoons of the butter in a large heavy pot and place it over medium-low heat. Sauté the onion until it turns a rich golden color.

2. Remove the rind and seeds from the squash, then cut it into ¾-inch cubes. When the onion is ready, add the squash to the pan with about ½ cup water and season with salt and pepper. Cook until the squash is tender and the water is evaporated, 10 to 15 minutes.

3. While the squash is cooking, heat the broth in a pot and keep it at a very low simmer.

4. When the squash is done, add the rice and stir until it is well coated. Add a couple ladlefuls of the heated broth and stir with a wooden spoon. Continue stirring and adding the broth gradually as the rice absorbs the liquid. Add just enough broth to produce the consistency of a rather thick soup. It is important to wait until all the liquid is absorbed each time before

adding more broth. The rice will be done in about 20 minutes, when it is firm to the bite but not still crunchy or chalky in the center. At the end, the risotto should have a creamy, almost "wavy" consistency.

5.   Remove the risotto from the heat. Stir in the parsley, Parmigiano-Reggiano, and the remaining 1 tablespoon butter. Taste for salt and serve at once.

SERVES 4 TO 6 PEOPLE

Red and Yellow Pepper Risotto

RISOTTO AI PEPERONI E POMODORO FRESCO

Sautéed onions with peppers and fresh tomatoes is a combination that always makes me lick my chops, whether it is with pasta, as a sauce for grilled or boiled meats, or in a risotto such as this one.

45 *minutes from start to finish*

⅓ cup finely chopped yellow onion
3 tablespoons butter
1 red bell pepper
1 yellow bell pepper
1 pound fresh, ripe plum tomatoes
Salt
Freshly ground black pepper

5 cups Homemade Meat Broth (page 45),
   or 1 large beef bouillon cube dissolved
   in 5 cups water
1½ cups rice for risotto, such as Arborio
   or Carnaroli
10 to 12 fresh basil leaves
⅓ cup freshly grated Parmigiano-Reggiano

1. Put the onion and 2 tablespoons of the butter in a large heavy pot and place it over medium-low heat. Sauté the onion until it turns a rich golden color.

2. While the onion is sautéing, peel the peppers (page 26) and remove the core and seeds. Cut the peppers into ½-inch squares.

3. When the onion is done, add the peppers and turn up the heat to medium-high. Sauté until the peppers begin to brown lightly, 8 to 10 minutes.

4. Peel the tomatoes (page 24), remove the seeds, and cut into ½-inch dice.

5. When the peppers have begun to brown, add the tomatoes, season with salt and pepper, and cook until all the water the tomatoes release evaporates.

6. Meanwhile, heat the broth in a pot and keep it at a very low simmer.

7. When the tomatoes are done, add the rice and stir until it is well coated. Add a couple ladlefuls of the heated broth and stir with a wooden spoon. Continue stirring and adding the broth gradually as the rice absorbs it. Add just enough broth to produce the consistency of a rather

thick soup. It is important to wait until all the liquid is absorbed each time before adding more broth. The rice will be done in about 20 minutes, when it is firm to the bite but not still crunchy or chalky in the center. At the end, the risotto should have a creamy, almost "wavy" consistency.

8. Remove from the heat. Tear the basil leaves into small pieces and stir them into the risotto along with the remaining 1 tablespoon butter and the Parmigiano-Reggiano and serve at once.

SERVES 4 TO 6 PEOPLE

Risotto with Shrimp and Asparagus
RISOTTO COI GAMBERI E ASPARAGI

Italian cooks have a special gift for combining vegetables with seafood. Zucchini and clams is a classic Neapolitan example. Shrimp and asparagus is also an inspired combination, as you will see when you try this risotto.

40-45 *minutes from start to finish*

8 ounces asparagus	8 ounces medium shrimp (31 to 40
Salt	per pound)
⅓ cup finely chopped yellow onion	1½ cups rice for risotto, such as Arborio
2 tablespoons extra-virgin olive oil, plus a	or Carnaroli
little extra for finishing the dish	Freshly ground black pepper

1. Choose a skillet that will accommodate the asparagus, fill it with water, and place over high heat. Trim about 1 inch from each asparagus stalk, then peel the remaining bottom third. When the water in the skillet comes to a boil, add about 1 teaspoon salt and the asparagus. Cook the asparagus until tender, 4 to 6 minutes.

2. While the asparagus is cooking, peel and finely chop the onion. Place it with the olive oil in a large, heavy pot over medium heat. Sauté until the onion turns a rich golden color.

3. When the asparagus is tender, use a pair of tongs to lift it out of the skillet and set aside. Pour the asparagus water into a pot and place it over low heat to keep it hot.

4. Peel the shrimp, devein if necessary, and cut them into approximately ½-inch pieces.

5. Cut the asparagus into 1-inch pieces and add them to the onion in the pot. Raise the heat to medium-high and sauté for 2 to 3 minutes. Add the rice and stir until it is well coated. Add a couple ladlefuls of the hot asparagus water and stir with a wooden spoon. Continue stirring and adding the asparagus water gradually as the rice absorbs the liquid. Add just enough water to produce the consistency of a rather thick soup. It is important to wait until all the liquid is absorbed each time before adding more water. When the rice is almost done (tender but still firm), after about 20 minutes, add the shrimp, which will only take about 2 minutes to

cook. If you use all the asparagus water before the rice is cooked, continue with heated plain water. When the risotto is done, it should have a creamy, almost "wavy" consistency.

6. Season with pepper, drizzle with a little olive oil, and taste for salt (usually the salt in the asparagus water will be sufficient). Serve at once.

SERVES 4 TO 6 PEOPLE

Baked Ham-and-Cheese Rice Casserole

RISO AL FORNO

This is a very easy dish that can be assembled as far in advance as the day before, then baked and served either as a single-course meal or as part of a dinner or buffet.

25-30 *minutes to prepare*

40-45 *minutes from start to finish*

Salt	Freshly ground pepper
1½ cups rice for risotto, such as Arborio or Carnaroli	6 ounces boiled ham, sliced fairly thin and chopped
4 tablespoons butter, plus more for the rice and the baking dish	¾ cup freshly grated Parmigiano-Reggiano
2 cups whole milk	6 ounces fresh mozzarella
¼ cup all-purpose flour	

1. Preheat the oven to 400°F.

2. Fill a pot with at least 3 quarts water and bring to a boil. Add about 2 teaspoons salt and the rice and stir well. Cook covered for about 15 minutes, stirring occasionally, until the rice is cooked but still firm to the bite (al dente). Drain and transfer to a mixing bowl. Toss the rice with a bit of butter to prevent the grains from sticking together.

3. While the rice is cooking, make a béchamel sauce. Heat the milk until you can see steam rising, being careful not to let it come to a boil. Melt the 4 tablespoons butter in a heavy saucepan over medium-low heat. Add the flour and whisk until smooth. Add the hot milk a few tablespoons at a time at first, whisking until the mixture is smooth before adding more milk. Do not be alarmed if the béchamel becomes very thick at first. It will get thinner as you whisk in more milk. Once it has become quite thin, you can pour the milk in more rapidly. Cook, whisking constantly, over medium-low heat until the sauce thickly coats the whisk. Season with salt and pepper before removing from the heat.

4. Pour the béchamel over the rice, reserving a few spoonfuls for the top of the casserole. Add the ham and all but 2 tablespoons of the Parmigiano-Reggiano. Mix well and taste for salt and pepper.

5. Butter the bottom and sides of a 2½-quart baking dish that is about 3½ inches deep. Pour in half of the rice mixture. Slice the mozzarella about ⅛ inch thick and layer the slices over the rice. Add the remaining rice mixture and smooth the surface with a spoon. Spread the remaining béchamel over the top and sprinkle with the remaining 2 tablespoons Parmigiano-Reggiano.

6. Bake for 15 minutes. If after 15 minutes the top is not speckled with brown, place the casserole under the broiler for 1 to 2 minutes, or until the top begins to brown. Remove from the oven and allow to settle for about 5 minutes before serving.

SERVES 4 TO 6 PEOPLE

The Un-Risotto

RISOTTO FINTO

This, of course, is not a risotto. It is not made by adding a little liquid at a time while constantly stirring and consequently does not have the creamy consistency of a classic risotto. It is, however, a delicious rice dish that is very easy to make and has the rich texture that a risotto-style rice, such as Arborio or Carnaroli, gives it.

25-30 *minutes from start to finish*

¼ cup finely chopped yellow onion

3 tablespoons butter

1½ cups rice for risotto, such as Arborio or Carnaroli

2¼ cups Homemade Meat Broth (page 45), or ½ large beef bouillon cube dissolved in 2¼ cups water

Salt

1 yellow bell pepper

4 ounces ground pork

1 cup diced peeled (page 24) fresh tomato

1 cup frozen tiny peas, thawed

Freshly ground black pepper

1. Put the onion and 1½ tablespoons of the butter in a large heavy pot over medium heat. Sauté until the onion turns a rich golden color. Add the rice and stir until it is well coated. Add the broth and a pinch of salt. Cover and cook at a steady simmer for 15 minutes.

2. While the rice is cooking, peel the bell pepper (page 26), remove the core and seeds, and cut it into long narrow strips.

3. Put the remaining 1½ tablespoons butter and the ground pork in a skillet over medium-high heat and cook until the pork is lightly browned. Add the bell pepper and continue cooking until it is tender.

4. While the pepper is cooking, peel and dice the tomato. When the pepper is done, add the tomato and peas. Season with salt and pepper. Cook for 5 to 8 minutes and remove from the heat.

5. Add the pork mixture to the rice and stir it in well. Cover the pot again and cook for 5 more minutes. Serve hot.

SERVES 4 TO 6 PEOPLE

Fish and Shellfish

Halibut Fillets Sautéed with Leeks and Red Peppers

FILETTI DI PESCE IN PADELLA CON PORRI E PEPERONI

The delicate flavors of leeks and red peppers complement each other in this simple and elegant fish dish.

30 *minutes from start to finish*

4 medium leeks (about 12 ounces)
4 tablespoons extra-virgin olive oil
Salt
Freshly ground black pepper
1 large red bell pepper

About ½ cup all-purpose flour (enough to coat the fish)
2 pounds halibut, sea bass, or other delicate, firm-fleshed fish fillets
⅓ cup dry white wine

1. Cut off the root ends of the leeks and trim the tough green tops of the leaves. Cut the leeks into about 2-inch lengths, then slice into narrow julienne strips. Place the cut leeks in a large bowl and cover with cold water. If they are very sandy, remove them, discard the dirty water, and cover again with fresh water.

2. Remove the leeks from the water. Put 2 tablespoons of the olive oil and the leeks in a sauté pan or skillet large enough to hold the fish fillets in a single layer and place it over medium-low heat. Add enough water to come about ½ inch up the side of the pan and season lightly with salt and pepper. Cover the pan and cook until the leeks are tender, about 10 minutes.

3. While the leeks are cooking, peel the red pepper (page 26) and remove the core and seeds. Cut the pepper into narrow lengthwise strips.

4. Add the red pepper to the leeks, raise the heat to medium-high, and sauté uncovered until the pepper is tender and the leeks are lightly browned, about 10 minutes. Remove the vegetables from the pan and set aside.

5. Add the remaining 2 tablespoons olive oil to the pan and heat it over medium-high heat. Put the flour on a plate, evenly coat the fish fillets with it, and shake off any excess. Test the oil in the pan with a drop of flour to see if it sizzles. When the oil is hot enough, add all the

fish to the pan and sauté, turning once, until both sides of the fish are lightly browned. Add the white wine, season the fish with salt and pepper, and put the vegetables back in the pan. Lower the heat to medium and cover the pan. Cook until the fish flakes easily when prodded with a fork or spatula, about 5 minutes longer. Remove the fish from the pan. If the sauce is too thin, reduce it over high heat until it coats a spoon thickly, then pour it over the fish. Serve at once.

SERVES 4 TO 6 PEOPLE

Pan-Roasted Pompano Fillets with Rosemary and Garlic

POMPANO AL ROSMARINO

Of the local fish available in Florida, one of my favorites is pompano. It is wonderful grilled whole or filleted and pan-roasted. If you cannot get pompano, try this recipe with mahi-mahi or even bluefish fillets.

15 *minutes from start to finish*

2 tablespoons extra-virgin olive oil
4 garlic cloves, lightly crushed and
    peeled
1 tablespoon coarsely chopped fresh
    rosemary leaves

1½ pounds pompano fillets, skin on
Salt
Freshly ground black pepper
2 tablespoons freshly squeezed lemon
    juice

1. Put the olive oil and garlic in a skillet or sauté pan large enough to accommodate the fish in a single layer and place it over medium-high heat. Sauté the garlic until the cloves are lightly browned on all sides, then remove and discard them.

2. Add the rosemary and fish fillets, skin side up. Sauté for 2 to 3 minutes, until the fish is lightly colored, then turn the fillets over and season with salt and pepper. Add the lemon juice and about ¼ cup water. Cover the pan and cook until the fish flakes easily when prodded with a fork, 5 to 6 minutes. Transfer the fish to a serving plate. If the juices in the pan are still watery, raise the heat to reduce them; if the pan is dry, add a little water and deglaze the pan to form a sauce. Pour the sauce over the fish and serve at once.

SERVES 4 TO 6 PEOPLE

Red Snapper with Fresh Tomatoes and Black Olives

PESCE AL POMODORO E OLIVE

This is almost a *Puttanesca* sauce for fish, without the anchovies. By cooking the fish in the sauce, the fillets soak up all the flavors. If you make the sauce ahead of time, you can cook and serve the fish in less than 15 minutes.

minutes from start to finish **25**

¾ cup finely chopped yellow onion
3 tablespoons extra-virgin olive oil
1 pound fresh, ripe tomatoes
2 teaspoons thinly sliced garlic
12 Kalamata olives

1½ tablespoons capers
2 pounds red snapper, striped bass, or
    grouper fillets
Salt
Freshly ground black pepper

1. Put the onion and olive oil in a skillet large enough to accommodate the fish fillets in a single layer and place it over medium-low heat. Sauté the onion until it turns a rich golden color.

2. While the onion is sautéing, peel the tomatoes (page 24) and, unless they are very ripe and flavorful, remove the seeds. Cut them into ½-inch dice.

3. When the onion is colored, add the garlic and cook, stirring, for about 1 minute. Add the tomatoes and cook until the water the tomatoes release evaporates by about half, about 10 minutes.

4. While the tomatoes cook, slice the olives by cutting the flesh away from the pits.

5. When the tomatoes are done, stir in the olives and capers. Put in the fish fillets and season with salt and pepper. Cover the pan and simmer over medium-low heat. The fish will take about 10 minutes per inch of thickness to cook. When it is about halfway done, turn the fillets over and check to see that there is still liquid in the pan. If all the liquid evaporates before the fish is done, add 2 tablespoons water. The fish is cooked when it flakes easily when prodded with a fork. Remove it from the pan with a slotted spatula. If the sauce is too watery, raise the heat and reduce it. Pour the sauce over the fish and serve at once.

SERVES 4 TO 6 PEOPLE

Salmon Fillets with a Caper and Anchovy Sauce

SALMONE AL SUGO DI ACCIUGHE

This is another example of how anchovies are used in Italian cooking to give a richness of flavor to a dish but not a strong fishy flavor. It is very important in this recipe to be patient and allow the onion to cook down slowly until it becomes very soft and almost caramelized. The result will be a rich, luscious sauce that perfectly complements salmon.

35–40 *minutes from start to finish*

2 cups very finely chopped yellow onion

4 tablespoons extra-virgin olive oil, plus more if needed

2 tablespoons finely chopped Italian flat-leaf parsley

6 anchovy fillets

⅓ cup dry white wine

1 tablespoon capers

About ¾ cup all-purpose flour (enough to coat the fish)

2 pounds skinless salmon fillets

Salt

Freshly ground black pepper

1. Put the onion and olive oil in a large skillet and place it over medium heat. Sauté the onion slowly, stirring occasionally, until it turns to a rich, but not too dark, caramel color. This will probably take about 20 minutes.

2. While the onion is cooking, chop the parsley and coarsely chop the anchovies.

3. When the onion is done, add the anchovies and mash them with a wooden spoon until they dissolve. Raise the heat to medium-high, then add the wine. Let it bubble until the wine is almost completely evaporated. Add the parsley and capers, cook for about 1 minute, and remove from the heat. Using a finely slotted spoon, remove the onion from the pan, leaving as much of the oil behind as possible. If there is not enough oil to coat the bottom of the pan completely, add a little more olive oil. Return the pan to medium-high heat.

4. Place the flour on a plate, evenly coat the salmon fillets with it, and shake off the excess. When the oil is hot enough to make the fillets sizzle, carefully slip them into the pan. Season

the fish with salt and pepper and cook until both sides are colored and the salmon flakes when prodded with a fork but is still moist in the center, 8 to 10 minutes.

5. When the salmon is done, pour the anchovy sauce back into the pan and turn the fish until it is well coated with the sauce. Serve at once.

N O T E : If you make the sauce ahead of time, remove the salmon from the pan, put in the sauce, and reheat it before coating the salmon with it.

SERVES 4 TO 6 PEOPLE

"Christmas Tree" Salmon

SALMONE "NATALIZIO"

Mara Martin and her husband, Maurizio, own Da Fiore, which is probably the best seafood restaurant in Venice, if not all of Italy. They are also good friends, and on a recent visit to Florida, Mara made this delicious dish for us and shared the recipe with me. It is very easy to do and, in addition to being very good, it is also very pretty. In fact, when you use the tail end of a fish fillet, it looks a little bit like a Christmas tree, hence the name I gave it.

15 *minutes to prepare*

40 *minutes from start to finish*

1 yellow bell pepper
1 red bell pepper
1 green bell pepper
2 tablespoons capers
¼ cup freshly grated Parmigiano-Reggiano
2 tablespoons plain fine dry bread crumbs

3 tablespoons extra-virgin olive oil, plus more for the baking dish
Salt
Freshly ground black pepper
1½ pounds salmon, striped bass, or sea bass fillet, skin on

1. Preheat the oven to 400°F.

2. Peel the peppers (page 26) and remove the core and seeds. Cut them into ¼-inch dice, to yield about ¾ cup of each pepper, and place them in a mixing bowl.

3. Add the capers, Parmigiano-Reggiano, bread crumbs, and olive oil and season with salt and pepper. Toss well.

4. Grease a baking dish large enough to accommodate the fish with a few drops of olive oil. Place the fish skin side down in it. Lightly season the fish with salt and pepper and cover it with the pepper mixture.

5. Bake until the fish is done, 20 to 25 minutes. It should flake when prodded with a fork but still be moist in the center or at the thickest part. The peppers should still be slightly crunchy. Serve at once.

SERVES 4 TO 6 PEOPLE

Thinly Sliced Sea Bass Marinated in Lemon (page 40)

Escarole, Bean, and Barley Soup (page 44)

Orecchiette with Fresh Tomato, Basil, and Ricotta Salata (page 75)

Butternut Squash Risotto (page 80)

Red Snapper with Fresh Tomatoes and Black Olives (page 93)

Fish Baked in Foil
with Juniper Berries (page 102)

Grilled Chicken Breast Stuffed with Asparagus and Fontina (page 112)

Chicken with Green Olives (page 120)

Sweet-and-Sour Braised Veal Shanks (page 132)

Rack of Lamb Encrusted with Parmesan Cheese (page 142)

Meat Pie, "Pizza" Style (page 156)

Artichoke and Potato Casserole (page 170)

Crunchy Salad (page 185)

Chicken Salad with Pomegranate, Pine Nuts, and Raisins (page 196)

Sicilian Orange Tart (page 200)

Glazed Peaches in White Wine (page 214)

Poached Fish with a Savory Green Sauce

PESCE LESSO CON SALSA VERDE

When you have a piece of very fresh fish, sometimes the best thing to do with it is as little as possible. Here the fish is poached and served either hot or at room temperature with a tasty caper and anchovy sauce. This is a perfect dish for a buffet.

minutes from start to finish 15–20

1 medium yellow onion, peeled and
    quartered
2 carrots, peeled and cut into 1½- to
    2-inch pieces
2 tablespoons red wine vinegar
Salt
2 pounds striped bass or snapper
    fillets

For the sauce:
8 anchovy fillets
¼ cup capers
¼ cup freshly squeezed lemon juice
¼ cup finely chopped Italian flat-leaf
    parsley
⅓ cup extra-virgin olive oil

1. Fill a pot large enough to hold the fish with water and put in the onion and carrots. Cover and bring to a boil over high heat. Add the vinegar and some salt. Put in the fish, adjust the heat so it simmers, and cook uncovered for about 10 minutes for each inch of thickness.

2. While the fish is cooking, put all the ingredients for the sauce in a food processor and let it run until the sauce is smooth and uniformly blended.

3. Carefully remove the cooked fish from the pot. Be certain the fish is done by seeing if it flakes when prodded with a fork before discarding the cooking water. Serve warm or at room temperature with the sauce on the side.

SERVES 4 TO 6 PEOPLE

Fresh Tuna Steaks with Marsala and Mushrooms

TONNO FRESCO AL MARSALA E FUNGHI

Often what we eat for dinner is what looks the freshest. One day while I perused the seafood case at the supermarket, a particularly good, fresh-looking piece of tuna caught my eye. In the produce department, I found some beautiful firm cremini mushrooms and thought to myself that they would be very good with that fresh tuna. Thus this recipe was conceived.

20 *minutes from start to finish*

½ cup yellow onion, thinly sliced lengthwise
3 tablespoons extra-virgin olive oil
8 ounces cremini or white mushrooms
Salt

Freshly ground black pepper
4 fresh, thick (¾ to 1 inch) tuna steaks (about 6 ounces each)
About ½ cup all-purpose flour (enough to coat the tuna)
3 tablespoons dry Marsala

1. Put the onion and 2 tablespoons of the olive oil in a large skillet and place it over medium heat. Sauté, stirring occasionally, until the onion turns a light caramel color, 3 to 5 minutes.

2. While the onion is sautéing, wipe the mushrooms clean with a soft mushroom brush or damp paper towel. Do not wash them, because they soak up water like a sponge. Trim the stems and thinly slice the mushrooms lengthwise.

3. When the onion is done, add the mushrooms and season with salt and pepper. Cook the mushrooms until all the water they release evaporates; this can take anywhere from 5 to 15 minutes. The goal is not to sear them but to let them cook slowly so that they become concentrated with flavor.

4. Remove the mushrooms and onion from the pan and set aside. Put the remaining 1 tablespoon olive oil in the pan and place it over high heat. Coat the tuna steaks with the flour and shake off the excess. When the oil is hot enough to make the fish sizzle, carefully slide in the tuna steaks. Do not overcrowd the pan. They should fit comfortably in a single layer; if nec-

essary, cook them in two batches. Cook 2 to 3 minutes on each side, depending on how rare you like your tuna. It should be at least pink in the middle, however, or it will be tough and dry. Set the seared tuna steaks on a platter and season them with salt and pepper.

5. Pour the Marsala into the hot skillet while it is still over high heat. Keep your face away from the pan in case the Marsala flames up. Stir with a wooden spoon to loosen all the tasty bits on the bottom of the pan.

6. Reduce the heat to medium-low and return the mushrooms and onion to the pan. Heat them through, add the tuna steaks, and turn them in the sauce just long enough to reheat them. Remove from the heat and serve at once.

SERVES 4 PEOPLE

Grilled Striped Bass Fillet, Adriatic Style

PESCE IN GRATICOLA ALL'ADRIATICA

Whenever I am with my parents and fresh fish and a grill are handy, they almost always ask me to make this recipe. My favorite fish to use is striped bass, but any fine white-fleshed fish, such as grouper or snapper, will work well. I prefer to use fillets rather than the whole fish because it allows the flavors in the marinade to penetrate more and makes it easier to judge when the fish is done. With very few exceptions (such as tuna), the only thing worse than overcooking fish is undercooking it. Remove the fish from the grill the moment you see the flesh begin to flake when prodded with a fork.

35 *minutes from start to finish*

2 tablespoons finely chopped Italian flat-leaf parsley
1 teaspoon finely chopped garlic
2 tablespoons plain fine dry bread crumbs
4 tablespoons extra-virgin olive oil

2 pounds striped bass fillets, skin on
Salt
Freshly ground black pepper
2 tablespoons freshly squeezed lemon juice

1. Combine the parsley, garlic, bread crumbs, and olive oil in a small bowl.

2. With a sharp knife, make diagonal slits about 1 inch apart in the skin of the fish. Season both sides of the fillets with salt and pepper. Place them on a platter, add the marinade, and turn the fish in it until it is well coated. Let it steep in the marinade for at least 15 minutes while you prepare the grill.

3. When the grill is very hot, put the fish skin side up on the grill. Cook until the side of the fish facing the fire turns golden brown. Turn the fillets, season with a little salt and pepper, and sprinkle with the lemon juice. (I find those double grills that hold the fish and allow you to turn it by simply turning the grill very useful.) Over a hot fire, the fish should cook for about 5 minutes per inch of thickness. The time will vary depending on how hot the grill is; the best way is to check it periodically with a fork (see note above). Serve at once.

SERVES 4 TO 6 PEOPLE

Whole Fish Baked in Salt

PESCE AL SALE

Do not let the fact that one of the first ingredients in this recipe is a whole box of kosher salt put you off. This is one of the most delicate, elegant, and easy-to-make fish dishes you are likely to encounter. The salt creates a protective shell around the fish and keeps the flesh incredibly moist and tender. The trick is to make sure to dry the fish well before covering it with the salt.

minutes to prepare **5**

minutes from start to finish **35–45**

2 very fresh cleaned whole fish, such as red snapper, yellowtail snapper, striped bass, or sea bass, weighing approximately 1½ to 2 pounds each and as close to the same size as possible

One 3-pound box kosher salt
Extra-virgin olive oil for serving

1. Preheat the oven to 400°F.

2. Rinse the fish well inside and out and pat them thoroughly dry with paper towels.

3. Cover the bottom of a baking dish large enough to accommodate both fish with a ½-inch layer of salt. Place the fish on it and cover them completely with the remaining salt.

3. Bake the fish for 30 to 40 minutes (calculate 20 minutes per pound). When it is done, take the fish out of the oven. Remove the top layer of salt by tapping it firmly with a spoon; it should come away in chunks. Gently lift out the fish and transfer it to a platter. Brush off any remaining salt, then fillet the fish and transfer to a serving platter. Drizzle a very small amount of extra-virgin olive oil over the fillets and serve at once.

SERVES 4 TO 6 PEOPLE

Fish Baked in Foil with Juniper Berries

PESCE AL CARTOCCIO COL GINEPRO

Juniper berries (also used to make gin) add a distinctive and delicate flavor to this dish. In this recipe the fish is baked sealed in aluminum foil with carrots, celery, and juniper berries. When it is done and you open the foil pouch, you will be rewarded with a mouthwatering waft of fragrant aromas.

20 *minutes to prepare*

40-60 *minutes from start to finish*

1 cup yellow onion, very thinly sliced crosswise
1 cup julienned carrots (⅛ inch thick and about 1 inch long)
¾ cup peeled, julienned celery (⅛ inch thick and about 1 inch long)
4 tablespoons extra-virgin olive oil
Salt

Freshly ground black pepper
2 pounds monkfish, grouper, halibut, or sea bass fillets (preferably no more than 1½ inches thick)
2 teaspoons juniper berries, lightly crushed with a mallet
¼ cup dry white wine

1. Preheat the oven to 450°F.

2. Put the onion, carrots, and celery in a sauté pan with 1 tablespoon of the olive oil and ¼ cup water. Season with salt and pepper and place the pan over medium-low heat. Cook until the onion is wilted and all the water evaporates, 10 to 15 minutes. Do not let the vegetables brown.

3. Line a baking pan large enough to hold the fish with a sheet of heavy-duty aluminum foil large enough to wrap around the fish completely. When you seal the foil later, there should be enough room around the fish for the steam to circulate while it bakes. Spread half of the cooked vegetables on the foil and place the fish over them. Salt and pepper the fish. Spoon

the remaining vegetables over the fish and add the juniper berries, white wine, and the remaining 3 tablespoons olive oil. Seal the pouch by folding and pinching the foil all around without leaving any openings, so the steam will not escape as it bakes.

4. Put the baking pan in the oven and bake until the fish is done. Delicate, thin fillets, such as halibut, will cook in about 20 minutes. Thicker fillets, such as grouper, may take about 30 minutes, and monkfish will need close to 40 minutes. To check the fish, carefully open the pouch just enough to slide a fork in. If the fish flakes, it is done. If not, reseal the pouch, bake for another 5 minutes, and try again. When it is done, gently open the foil, keeping the pouch away from your face, as the steam inside will be very hot. Taking care not to spill the juices, lift the pouch out of the baking pan and slide the fish, vegetables, and juices onto a serving dish. Serve at once.

SERVES 4 TO 6 PEOPLE

Devil's Shrimp with Brandy and Fresh Tomatoes

I GAMBERI DEL DIAVOLO

These shrimp are named after the devil because they are spicy (more or less so depending on how devilish you feel) and because it is possible to flame them when the brandy is added. The purpose of flaming is to cook off the alcohol, but it is more of a show than a requirement since, over high heat, the alcohol evaporates anyway.

35-40 *minutes from start to finish*

1½ pounds large shrimp (21 to 25 per pound)

12 ounces fresh, ripe plum tomatoes

2 tablespoons very thinly sliced garlic

3 tablespoons extra-virgin olive oil

¼ teaspoon crushed red pepper flakes, or to taste

2 tablespoons brandy or grappa

Salt

1. Peel the shrimp and devein them if necessary.

2. Peel the tomatoes (page 24), remove the seeds, and cut into narrow strips.

3. Put the garlic and olive oil in a skillet large enough to accommodate the shrimp in a single layer and place it over high heat. Sauté the garlic until it begins to sizzle. Add the red pepper flakes and shrimp and sauté very briefly until both sides of the shrimp begin to change color. Add the brandy and flame it, or cook it for about 10 seconds to evaporate the alcohol. (Flaming is best done on a gas stove. After adding the brandy, move the skillet so that the edge is over the center of the burner and tip the pan slightly toward the flame. Be sure to stand back to avoid getting burned.)

4. Add the tomatoes and season with salt. Cook, stirring, until the shrimp are done, 2 to 3 minutes. Do not overcook the shrimp, or they will become tough. Serve at once.

SERVES 4 TO 6 PEOPLE

Shrimp Broiled with Rosemary

GAMBERONI AL FORNO

In the famous town of Portofino on the Italian Riviera, there is a restaurant called Puny (I sincerely doubt the owners are aware of the meaning of the word in English), and the food served there is quite extraordinary. One of the dishes I had was jumbo shrimp baked with lemon and fresh rosemary. It is ridiculously simple to prepare yet utterly delicious. Of course, one needs the best-looking shrimp possible and an excellent extra-virgin olive oil.

minutes from start to finish **20**

1½ pounds extra-large shrimp
(16 to 20 per pound)
¼ cup freshly squeezed lemon juice
4 tablespoons extra-virgin olive oil

2 tablespoons chopped fresh
rosemary leaves
Salt
Freshly ground black pepper

1. Preheat the broiler.

2. Devein the shrimp without peeling them by cutting the shell along the back with a pair of scissors and making a shallow slit in the flesh with a paring knife. Place the shrimp in a shallow baking dish in which they will fit comfortably in a single layer. Add the lemon juice, olive oil, and rosemary; season with salt and pepper. Toss the shrimp well and spread them in the dish. Broil the shrimp for 5 minutes, turn them over, and broil until the shrimp are pink throughout, 2 to 4 minutes more.

3. Before serving, toss the shrimp in the juices that will have formed, adding another light sprinkling of salt. The best way to eat them is to put the baking dish in the middle of the table and have everybody take one shrimp at a time, peel it, and dip it into the juices in the pan.

SERVES 4 PEOPLE AS A MAIN DISH OR 6 TO 8 PEOPLE AS AN APPETIZER

Shrimp and Beans

GAMBERI COI FAGIOLI

I don't know why, but shrimp and beans make a perfect combination. Here a little pancetta is added, which makes the dish particularly tasty. This recipe is prepared in two easy stages, and the beans can easily be made ahead of time using canned beans. The shrimp are cooked at the last minute and will be done in the time it takes for the beans to reheat.

30 *minutes from start to finish*

1 cup yellow onion, thinly sliced crosswise	6 to 8 fresh sage leaves
4 tablespoons extra-virgin olive oil	4 garlic cloves, lightly crushed and peeled
2 ounces pancetta, sliced about ¼ inch thick	3 tablespoons dry white wine
1 pound large shrimp (21 to 25 per pound)	2 teaspoons finely chopped Italian flat-leaf parsley
1½ cups drained canned cranberry or cannellini beans	Salt
	Freshly ground black pepper

1. Put the onion and 2 tablespoons of the olive oil in a large skillet or sauté pan and place it over medium heat. Sauté until the onion turns a rich golden color.

2. While the onion is sautéing, unravel the pancetta and cut it into strips about 1 inch long and ⅛ inch thick. Peel and devein the shrimp.

3. Add the pancetta to the onion and cook until it begins to color lightly. Then add the beans and sage and cook for 3 to 4 minutes. Remove from the heat and set aside.

4. When you are ready to serve, put the garlic and the remaining 2 tablespoons olive oil in a clean large skillet and place it over high heat. Begin reheating the beans over low heat if necessary. Sauté the garlic until it begins to color, then remove the cloves and discard them. Add the shrimp and sauté for about 1 minute. Add the wine and parsley and season with salt and pepper. Cook the shrimp until they turn completely pink, about 2 to 3 minutes.

5. Toss the hot beans and the shrimp together and serve at once with good crusty bread.

SERVES 4 TO 6 PEOPLE AS A MAIN DISH OR 8 PEOPLE AS AN APPETIZER

Grilled Soft-Shell Crabs, Adriatic Style

GRANCHI IN GRATICOLA

I was visiting my parents, who had rented a house on Long Island one summer, when I spotted some soft-shell crabs at their favorite fish market. I was reminded of a delicious dish of fried tiny soft-shell crabs I had eaten in Venice, and we rushed home to see if I could reproduce the dish with American crabs. Unfortunately the result was disappointing, but my father suggested I buy another batch and grill them Adriatic style with parsley, garlic, bread crumbs, and olive oil. They were a big hit, and we all agreed this is one of the most delectable ways to prepare soft-shell crabs.

minutes to prepare **15**

minutes from start to finish **30**

2 tablespoons finely chopped Italian
    flat-leaf parsley
1 teaspoon finely chopped garlic
2 tablespoons plain fine dry bread
    crumbs
⅓ cup extra-virgin olive oil

Salt
Freshly ground black pepper
6 cleaned soft-shell crabs
2 tablespoons freshly squeezed lemon
    juice

1. Combine the parsley, garlic, bread crumbs, and olive oil; season with salt and pepper. Turn the crabs in the mixture, coating them well. Allow to marinate for 10 to 15 minutes while you light the grill and get a good fire going.

2. When the grill is ready, arrange the rack about 3 inches from the coals. (If you are using a gas grill, set the flame on medium.) Put the crabs on the rack and grill until browned on one side, 2 to 3 minutes. Turn them over and sprinkle the lemon juice over them. Brown the second side, remove them from the grill, and serve at once.

SERVES 6 PEOPLE

Meats

Boneless Breast of Chicken with Three Peppers

PETTI DI POLLO TRICOLORE

My mother makes a delicious sauce for pasta with red, green, and yellow peppers and cream that I have adapted for chicken breasts. The preparation time given here is for boneless chicken breasts. If you do not mind spending an extra 15 minutes, buy three whole chicken breasts and bone them following the instructions on page 30. You will get the choicest part of the breast, the tenderloin, and bones that you can use to make a fine chicken broth, not to mention the fact that you will save money at the supermarket.

25 minutes from start to finish

¾ cup finely chopped yellow onion
3 tablespoons butter
2 tablespoons vegetable oil
1 cup diced (¼ inch) green bell peppers
1 cup diced (¼ inch) red bell peppers
1 cup diced (¼ inch) yellow bell peppers (if unavailable, use 2 cups diced red peppers)

Salt
Freshly ground black pepper
1½ pounds boneless, skinless chicken breasts (approximately 2 pounds bone-in; see page 30 for boning instructions)
½ cup heavy cream
2 tablespoons finely chopped Italian flat-leaf parsley

1. Put the onion, 2 tablespoons of the butter, and 1 tablespoon of the vegetable oil in a large skillet or sauté pan and place it over medium heat. Sauté the onion until it turns a rich golden color.

2. While the onion is sautéing, dice the peppers. When the onion has turned golden, raise the heat to medium-high and add all the peppers. Season with salt and pepper and cook, stirring occasionally, until the peppers are tender and begin to brown lightly.

3. While the peppers are cooking, fillet the chicken breasts: trim all the fat and any cartilage attached to the chicken breasts. Slice them horizontally in half, or thirds if the breasts are large, to get thin fillets (page 32).

4. Put the remaining butter and vegetable oil in a large skillet or sauté pan over high heat. When the butter foam begins to subside, carefully slide in as many chicken fillets as will comfortably fit in the pan without overlapping. Cook on each side until it begins to brown, then transfer the chicken to a platter. Be careful not to cook the chicken much more than about 1 minute on each side, or it will become dry. It will have a chance to cook a little longer with the sauce at the end. When all the chicken is done, season it with salt and pepper. Keep the pan over high heat and add about ¼ cup water. Scrape the bottom of the pan with a wooden spoon to loosen all the tasty brown bits and let the liquid bubble away until it is reduced to a saucelike consistency and set aside.

5. When the peppers are tender and lightly colored, add the deglazing liquid from the pan the chicken browned in, heavy cream, and parsley. Cook until the liquid has reduced by about half. Add the chicken fillets and turn them in the sauce until they are heated through and well coated. Serve at once.

SERVES 4 TO 6 PEOPLE

Grilled Chicken Breast Stuffed with Asparagus and Fontina

PETTI DI POLLO ALLA GUIDO RENI

Guido Reni was an early-seventeenth-century Bolognese painter and a master of the classical baroque style. The dish is named after him because of its colorful and sumptuous qualities. The original Bolognese dish is made with a veal chop. This is my version, made with chicken instead. I find the filling gives the chicken a wonderful flavor while keeping it very moist.

25 *minutes from start to finish*

8 asparagus spears
Salt
2 boneless, skinless chicken breasts
    (approximately 1½ pounds bone-in;
    see page 30 for boning instructions)

4 ounces fontina cheese
1 small vine-ripened tomato, or
    2 fresh, ripe plum tomatoes
8 fresh basil leaves
Freshly ground black pepper

1. Light the grill.

2. Fill a skillet or sauté pan large enough to hold the asparagus with water and place it over high heat.

3. Cut off the tough white part at the bottom of the asparagus spears, then peel the bottom third. When the water in the skillet is boiling, add some salt and slide in the asparagus. Cook until tender, about 5 minutes, then remove from the water and set aside.

4. While the asparagus is cooking, trim all the fat and any cartilage attached to the chicken breasts. Butterfly each half by slicing it horizontally in half, without cutting all the way through to the other side, so that the breast opens like a book.

5. Cut the fontina into thin slices and place a layer over the inside of one of the flaps of each butterflied chicken breast. Peel the tomato (page 24), slice it, and place the slices over the cheese. Put 2 asparagus spears, cut in half, on top of the tomato on each chicken breast. Add 2 basil leaves to each and season lightly with salt. Bring the top flap over to close each breast and secure it with toothpicks.

6. Place the stuffed chicken breasts on the hot grill and cook for 5 to 6 minutes on each side. Season with salt and pepper when turning them over. Serve at once.

N O T E : You can stuff the chicken several hours ahead of time. Cover it with plastic and keep it in the refrigerator until you are ready to cook it.

SERVES 4 PEOPLE

Chicken Breast Fillets with Red and Yellow Peppers

PETTI DI POLLO ALLA CAMPAGNOLA

Campagnola in Italian means "of the country," and this dish has rustic flavors and lots of vegetables. It can be put together very quickly if you prepare the vegetables ahead of time.

45 *minutes from start to finish*

3 cups yellow onion, very thinly sliced crosswise
4 tablespoons extra-virgin olive oil
1 yellow bell pepper
1 red bell pepper
1½ pounds fresh, ripe tomatoes
Salt
Freshly ground black pepper
20 Kalamata olives

1 teaspoon fresh oregano leaves
2 tablespoons finely chopped Italian flat-leaf parsley
1½ pounds boneless, skinless chicken breasts (approximately 2 pounds bone-in; see page 30 for boning instructions)
Vegetable oil

1. Put the onion and olive oil in a large skillet and place it over medium-low heat. Sauté until the onion turns a rich golden color.

2. While the onion is sautéing, peel the peppers (page 26) and remove the core and seeds. Cut into strips about ¼ inch wide. When the onion is done, add the peppers and raise the heat to medium. Cook until the peppers are almost completely tender.

3. While the peppers are cooking, peel the tomatoes (page 24) and coarsely chop them. Add them to the skillet and season with salt and pepper. Raise the heat to medium-high and cook until all the liquid in the pan evaporates.

4. While the tomatoes are cooking, cut the olives into slivers by cutting the flesh away from the pits. Chop the oregano. When the sauce is ready, add the olives, oregano, and parsley and cook for about 1 minute (see Note). Transfer to a bowl and set aside. Set the skillet aside.

5. Trim all the fat and any cartilage from the chicken breasts. Slice the chicken breasts horizontally to obtain thin fillets (page 32). Put the skillet over high heat and add a little vegetable oil to coat the bottom of the pan. When the oil is hot, add the chicken in batches so as not to crowd the pan, cook briefly on both sides, and transfer to a platter. Take care not to overcook the chicken or it will become dry and tough. When all the chicken is done, season it with salt and pepper. Deglaze the skillet with any juices the chicken released onto the platter and some water if necessary. Add the sauce and heat it through. Add the chicken fillets and turn them in the sauce until they are well coated. Serve at once.

N O T E : If you prepare the sauce ahead of time, don't add the olives, oregano, and parsley until you reheat the sauce just before adding the chicken.

SERVES 6 PEOPLE

Chicken Breast Fillets with Porcini Mushrooms

PETTI DI POLLO ALLA BOSCAIOLA

This is a version of Chicken Braised with Porcini Mushrooms (page 122), with boneless chicken breast fillets instead of chicken parts. The sauce can easily be prepared ahead of time so that all that needs to be done at the last minute is to sauté the chicken.

45 *minutes from start to finish*

1 ounce dried porcini mushrooms	Freshly ground black pepper
½ cup finely chopped yellow onion	1 pound boneless, skinless chicken
2 tablespoons butter	breasts (approximately 2 pounds
⅓ cup drained canned whole peeled	bone-in; see page 30 for boning
tomatoes, coarsely chopped	instructions)
Salt	1 tablespoon vegetable oil

1. Soak the dried mushrooms in a bowl with 1 cup lukewarm water until they soften, at least 10 minutes. Lift them out and squeeze the excess water back into the bowl. Rinse them under cold running water and coarsely chop them. Filter the soaking water through a paper towel or coffee filter and set aside.

2. While the mushrooms are soaking, put the onion and 1 tablespoon of the butter in a large sauté pan and place it over medium heat. Sauté the onion until it turns a light caramel color. Add the porcini mushrooms and the soaking water. Raise the heat to high and cook until almost all the liquid evaporates. Add the tomatoes and season with salt and pepper. Reduce the heat to medium and continue cooking until the sauce is reduced and no longer watery, 10 to 15 minutes. Remove the pan from the heat.

3. Trim all the fat and any cartilage from the chicken breasts. Slice the breasts horizontally to obtain thin fillets (page 32). Put the remaining 1 tablespoon butter and the vegetable oil in a large skillet and place it over high heat. When the butter foam begins to subside and the oil is nice and hot, carefully slide in the chicken fillets in batches, so as not to crowd the pan. Cook the fillets briefly on both sides and transfer to a platter. Take care not to overcook the

chicken, or it will become dry and tough. When all the chicken is done, season it with salt and pepper.

4. When you are ready to serve, reheat the chicken fillets together with the sauce. As soon as the chicken is heated through, remove the pan from the heat and serve at once. Do not let the chicken heat in the pan too long, or it will dry out.

SERVES 4 PEOPLE

Chicken Breast Fillets Rolled with Pancetta, Rosemary, and Sage

PETTI DI POLLO ARROTOLATI

This is a tasty and very quick way to cook chicken breasts. I prefer to cut the chicken breasts rather than pound them to get thinner slices because I find that chicken is a delicate meat and pounding breaks up its fibers.

15 *minutes to prepare*

35 *minutes from start to finish*

2 large or 3 small whole boneless, skin-less chicken breasts (approximately 2 to 2½ pounds bone-in; see page 30 for boning instructions)

4 teaspoons chopped fresh rosemary leaves

4 teaspoons chopped fresh sage leaves

12 thin slices (not paper-thin) pancetta

Salt

Freshly ground black pepper

1 tablespoon butter

1 tablespoon vegetable oil

¼ cup dry white

1. Preheat the oven to 400°F.

2. Trim all the fat and any cartilage attached to the chicken breasts. Cut them horizontally, in half if they are small or in 3 pieces if they are large, to get a total of 12 thin fillets (page 32).

3. Lay the chicken fillets flat and sprinkle the herbs over them. Put a slice of pancetta over each fillet, then roll it up and tie it with kitchen twine. Lightly season with salt and pepper (bear in mind that the pancetta is quite salty).

4. Put the butter and vegetable oil in a baking pan. Turn the chicken rolls in the oil to coat them, then bake for 10 minutes. Turn the rolls, add the white wine, and bake for another 10 minutes. Check to see if the chicken is done by piercing it and making sure the juices run clear. Remove the chicken from the pan, remove the twine, and arrange the rolls on a serving platter. If the juices in the pan are still quite runny (which they usually are), transfer them to a small skillet and reduce them over high heat. Pour them over the chicken and serve.

SERVES 4 TO 6 PEOPLE

Chicken Braised with Red Wine

POLLO AL CHIANTI

Looking for a bargain fare to Italy? Close your eyes as you take your first bite, and the flavors of this dish will take you to a farm on the hills of Tuscany in the heart of Chianti country.

minutes to prepare **15**

minutes from start to finish **60**

1 frying chicken (3½ to 4 pounds)	2 teaspoons thinly sliced garlic
2 tablespoons extra-virgin olive oil	1 teaspoon chopped fresh rosemary leaves
Salt	1 teaspoon chopped fresh sage leaves
Freshly ground black pepper	½ cup Chianti or robust dry red wine

1. Rinse the chicken and cut it into 10 pieces: 2 wings, 2 drumsticks, 2 thighs, and 4 breast pieces. Put the olive oil in a large sauté pan that can accommodate the chicken snugly and place the pan over high heat. Pat the chicken pieces dry with paper towels. When the oil is hot, carefully slip in half of the chicken pieces and brown them on all sides. Transfer the browned chicken to a platter and brown the rest of the chicken. When all the chicken is browned, season it with salt and pepper and remove the pan from the heat.

2. While the chicken is browning, slice the garlic and chop the fresh herbs. Once the pan is off the heat, put in the garlic and herbs and stir for about 30 seconds. Return the pan to high heat and add the red wine. Let it bubble for about 30 seconds to evaporate the alcohol, then reduce the heat to medium-low. Return all the chicken to the pan. Cover the pan with the lid slightly askew. Cook at a moderate simmer until the chicken is tender and comes off the bone easily, about 45 minutes. If all the liquid in the pan evaporates before the chicken is done, add a little water. When the chicken is done, remove it from the pan. If the sauce is too thin, reduce it until it coats a spoon; if it is too dry, add a little water and then reduce it. Pour the sauce over the chicken and serve.

NOTE: Like most braised dishes, this is just as good 1 or 2 days later. To reheat it, put the chicken back in the same pan with its sauce and a little water over low heat.

SERVES 4 PEOPLE

Chicken with Green Olives

POLLO ALLE OLIVE VERDI

This is probably the first recipe of mine that was published. It appeared in my mother's third book, *Marcella's Italian Kitchen,* in which she tells how on one of my visits home, I volunteered to cook and, after poking around my parents' refrigerator and cupboards, came up with this chicken dish. I confess that my memory of the first time I made it is rather vague, but I have been preparing it often to rave reviews over the years, during which time I have made some adjustments to the recipe. The following is my current version.

20 *minutes to prepare*

60 *minutes from start to finish*

8 ounces green olives, preferably Sicilian, slivered by cutting the flesh away from the pits

5 anchovy fillets

2 tablespoons extra-virgin olive oil

4 garlic cloves, lightly crushed and peeled

3 pounds chicken legs, thighs, and wings

Salt

Freshly ground black pepper

½ cup dry white wine

3 tablespoons red wine vinegar

3 tablespoons freshly squeezed lemon juice

2 tablespoons finely chopped Italian flat-leaf parsley

1. Put half the olives and all the anchovy fillets in a food processor and chop very fine.

2. Choose a lidded sauté pan or skillet large enough to accommodate all the chicken in a single layer. Put the olive oil and garlic in the pan and place it over medium-high heat. Sauté until the garlic turns golden brown, then remove the cloves and discard them.

3. Raise the heat to high, pat the chicken pieces dry with a paper towel, and place them skin side down in the pan. Brown the chicken on all sides, then transfer it to a platter and season it with salt and pepper.

4. Pour off most of the fat in the pan, then add the wine and vinegar. Let it bubble away until it is reduced by almost half, while loosening the tasty bits at the bottom of the pan with a

wooden spoon. Add the anchovy and olive mixture and about 2 tablespoons water. Return the chicken to the pan and turn the pieces in the sauce. Lower the heat to medium-low and cover the pan with the lid slightly askew. Cook, turning the chicken occasionally, until it is very tender when pricked with a fork, 35 to 40 minutes. If all the liquid in the pan evaporates before the chicken is done, add a little water.

5. When the chicken is done, uncover the pan. If the sauce is too thin and watery, raise the heat to let it reduce. With the heat on medium-low, add the remaining olives, the lemon juice, and parsley and cook for 1 to 2 minutes longer. Remove from the heat and serve hot.

NOTE : The chicken may be prepared up to a day ahead of time through step 4. When you are ready to serve it, reheat it over low heat, adding the remaining olives, the lemon juice, and parsley and a little water if necessary.

SERVES 4 TO 6 PEOPLE

Chicken Braised with Porcini Mushrooms

POLLO AI PORCINI SECCHI

Dried porcini mushrooms that are of very good quality bestow a rich wild mushroom flavor to a dish without overpowering it. Chicken braised with premium dried porcini becomes enveloped in their lush flavor and texture.

20 *minutes to prepare*

60 *minutes from start to finish*

1 ounce dried porcini mushrooms
1 frying chicken (3 to 3½ pounds)
2 tablespoons vegetable oil
Salt
Freshly ground black pepper
1 cup yellow onion, thinly sliced crosswise
2 tablespoons butter

3 ounces pancetta, sliced ¼ inch thick, cut into strips 1 inch long and ⅛ inch thick
1 pound fresh, ripe tomatoes
1½ tablespoons finely chopped Italian flat-leaf parsley

1. Soak the dried mushrooms in enough water to cover until softened, 15 to 20 minutes.

2. Rinse the chicken and cut it into 10 pieces: 2 wings, 2 drumsticks, 2 thighs, and 4 breast pieces. Put the vegetable oil in a 10- to 12-inch sauté pan and place it over high heat. When the oil is hot, pat the chicken pieces dry with a paper towel and carefully slip them into the pan. (Do not overcrowd the pan; if necessary, brown the chicken in batches.) Brown the chicken on all sides, transfer to a platter, and season with salt and pepper. Discard the oil in the pan.

3. While the chicken is browning, slice the onion. When all the chicken is done, put the butter and onion in the sauté pan and place it over medium-low heat. Sauté until the onion is wilted and begins to turn a golden color.

4. While the onion is sautéing, slice the pancetta and peel (page 24) and coarsely chop the tomatoes. When the onion is ready, add the pancetta and turn the heat up to medium-high. Cook until the pancetta becomes lightly colored.

5. While the pancetta is cooking, lift the soaked porcini out of the water and squeeze the excess water back into the bowl. Rinse the mushrooms under cold water. Coarsely chop them, then add them to the onion and pancetta. Add the soaking water, pouring it into the pan through a paper towel to trap any sand.

6. Cook until the liquid is almost completely evaporated. Add the chopped tomatoes and parsley and season with salt and pepper. Put in all the chicken except the breast pieces. Cook with the cover slightly askew over medium heat for about 25 minutes, turning the chicken once or twice. Add the breast pieces and continue cooking for another 15 to 20 minutes, depending on the size of the pieces. If all the liquid in the pan evaporates before the chicken is done, add 3 to 4 tablespoons water.

N O T E : This dish can be prepared 2 to 3 days ahead of time and reheated gently over low heat. I find that sometimes it tastes even better after a day or two.

SERVES 4 PEOPLE

Chicken Braised with Tomatoes and Black Olives

POLLO AL POMODORO E OLIVE

This recipe is a good example of how anchovies are used in Italian cooking. Because they are added at the beginning of the cooking process, they become virtually unnoticeable by the time the dish is done. Without them, however, the sauce would never have the depth of flavor only anchovies can give.

15-20 *minutes to prepare*

60 *minutes from start to finish*

1 frying chicken (3½ to 4 pounds)	1½ cups canned whole peeled tomatoes with their juice, coarsely chopped
2 tablespoons extra-virgin olive oil	
Salt	10 Kalamata olives, slivered by cutting the flesh away from the pits
Freshly ground black pepper	
6 anchovy fillets, chopped	2 tablespoons finely chopped Italian flat-leaf parsley
2 teaspoons finely chopped garlic	

1. Rinse the chicken and cut it into 10 pieces: 2 wings, 2 drumsticks, 2 thighs, and 4 breast pieces. Choose a sauté pan large enough to hold the chicken pieces snugly, even slightly overlapped if necessary. Put 1 tablespoon of the olive oil in the pan and place it over high heat. Pat the chicken pieces dry with a paper towel. When the oil is hot, carefully slip in half the chicken pieces. Brown them on all sides and transfer to a platter. Repeat with the rest of the chicken. When all the chicken has browned, season with salt and pepper. Remove the pan from the heat.

2. Pour off most of the fat in the pan and add the remaining 1 tablespoon olive oil. Place the pan over medium heat, add the anchovies, and stir until they begin to dissolve. Add the garlic and allow it to sizzle for just a few moments. Add the tomatoes and season lightly with salt and pepper. Return all of the chicken except for the breast pieces to the pan. When the tomatoes start bubbling, adjust the heat to a moderate but steady simmer. Cover the pan, leaving

the lid slightly askew. Cook for about 25 minutes. Add the breast pieces and cook for another 15 to 20 minutes, until the chicken feels very tender when prodded with a fork. Turn the chicken pieces occasionally as they cook, and if all the liquid evaporates before the chicken is done, add a little water.

3. When the chicken is done, add the olives and parsley and cook for 2 more minutes before serving.

NOTE: This dish can easily be prepared ahead of time. Do not add the olives and the parsley until you reheat it and are ready to serve.

SERVES 4 TO 6 PEOPLE

Turkey Breast Fillets with Lemon and Olives

PETTO DI TACCHINO ALLE OLIVE

I am not a big fan of turkey, but I was very pleased with the way this recipe turned out. You can serve it right away or let it stand for an hour or more and reheat it before serving. The flavors of the sauce will permeate the turkey fillets, making them taste even better. I reheat this, covered, in the microwave, so that it doesn't dry out.

20-25 *minutes from start to finish*

3 tablespoons extra-virgin olive oil
1¾ pounds turkey breast, sliced
    horizontally into ¼-inch-thick
    fillets (page 32)
About ½ cup all-purpose flour (enough
    to coat the turkey fillets)
Salt

Freshly ground black pepper
5 anchovy fillets, coarsely chopped
⅓ cup freshly squeezed lemon juice
12 black Greek olives, slivered by
    cutting the flesh away from
    the pits
3 bay leaves

1. Put 2 tablespoons of the olive oil in a large skillet and place it over high heat. Coat the turkey fillets with the flour and shake off the excess. When the oil is hot, slip in a few of the turkey fillets and cook them briefly on both sides. Transfer to a platter. Cook the remaining fillets in batches so as not to overcrowd the pan. After it is cooked, season the turkey with salt and pepper.

2. Lower the heat to medium and add the remaining 1 tablespoon olive oil and the anchovies. Mash the anchovies with a wooden spoon until they begin to dissolve. Add the lemon juice, olives, and bay leaves. Cook for about 1 minute. Return the turkey fillets to the pan and turn to coat them with the sauce. Serve right away, or let stand for up to 3 hours and reheat the fillets in the sauce before serving.

SERVES 4 TO 6 PEOPLE

Sage-Scented Grilled Veal Chops

COSTOLETTE DI VITELLO AI FERRI

When you want to have something special and spend very little time making it, a succulent grilled veal chop is just the thing. Here a beautiful chop is briefly marinated with extra-virgin olive oil and sage and grilled. A simple salad and a bottle of Brunello di Montalcino or Chianti Classico Riserva are all you need to complete the meal.

minutes from start to finish **25**

4 veal loin or rib chops, at least
    1 inch thick
2 tablespoons fresh sage leaves
2 tablespoons extra-virgin olive oil, plus
    some for brushing at the end

Salt
Freshly ground black pepper

1. Light the grill.

2. Place the chops on a platter. Cut the sage leaves into thin strips. Sprinkle the olive oil and sage over the veal and turn the meat until it is well coated on all sides.

3. When the grill is very hot, put on the chops and cook for about 5 minutes. Turn them over, season with salt and pepper, and grill for 3 to 5 minutes longer for medium-rare, depending on how hot the grill is. Remove from the grill and brush with some fresh olive oil. Serve at once.

SERVES 4 PEOPLE

Veal Stew with Green and Yellow Peppers

SPEZZATINO DI VITELLO COI PEPERONI

This colorful and satisfying stew is very good served with rice or with potatoes, either roasted or boiled. Yellow peppers, being the sweetest, and green peppers, the tartest, contrast with each other wonderfully in the dish.

20 *minutes to prepare*

90 *minutes from start to finish*

3 tablespoons butter
1 tablespoon vegetable oil
2 pounds boneless veal shoulder, cut into 1-inch pieces
Salt
Freshly ground black pepper

⅓ cup finely chopped yellow onion
1½ cups canned whole peeled tomatoes with their juice, coarsely chopped
2 green bell peppers
2 yellow bell peppers
½ cup heavy cream

1. Put the butter and vegetable oil in a sauté or braising pan at least 2 inches deep and large enough to hold the veal snugly but not necessarily in a single layer. Place it over high heat. When the butter foam begins to subside and the fat is hot enough to sizzle when tested with a bit of the veal, add as much veal as will comfortably fit in the pan in a single layer and lightly brown the meat on all sides. Transfer it to a platter. Repeat with the remaining veal. Season with salt and pepper.

2. Remove the pan from the heat and add the onion. The pan will probably retain enough heat to sauté the onion, but if necessary, place it over medium heat. Sauté until the onion turns a light brown color.

3. Add the tomatoes, season them with a little salt and pepper, and return all the meat to the pan. When the tomatoes begin bubbling, adjust the heat so that the stew is cooking at a gentle simmer. Put the lid on slightly askew and cook until the meat is tender, 1 to 1½ hours, depending on the quality of the veal. Stir the stew every 20 minutes or so and check that

there is still enough liquid in the pan. If the liquid evaporates before the meat is done, add a little water.

4. While the meat is cooking, peel the peppers (page 26) and remove the core, pith, and seeds. Cut the peppers into strips about 1 inch long and ½ inch wide. When the veal is tender, add the peppers and cover the pan completely. Continue cooking until the peppers are tender, about 15 minutes. Add the cream, stir for about 1 minute, and serve.

N O T E : The stew can be prepared 2 to 3 days in advance through step 3. About 20 minutes before serving, reheat the stew and proceed with step 4.

SERVES 4 TO 6 PEOPLE

Pan-Roasted Veal Stuffed with Spinach

ARROSTO DI VITELLO RIPIENO DI SPINACI

This rather impressive sounding dish is actually quite easy to prepare, and once it goes on the stove requires very little attention. I prefer using the breast of veal because it is a moister and more succulent cut, but if you prefer a leaner cut, you can use the shoulder instead. Ask the butcher to open it up for you so that you can stuff it with the spinach.

25 *minutes to prepare*

2 *hours from start to finish*

10 ounces fresh spinach
Salt
2 pounds boned veal breast (if you pur-
    chase the breast bone-in, it should
    weigh about 4 pounds)
4 large garlic cloves, peeled
2 tablespoons butter

1 tablespoon vegetable oil
Freshly ground black pepper
⅓ cup dry white wine
1 cup coarsely chopped peeled (page
    24) fresh, ripe tomatoes, or 1 cup
    coarsely chopped canned whole
    peeled tomatoes with their juice

1. Remove any large, thick stems from the spinach and rinse the leaves in cold water. Put the spinach in a pot with just the water that clings to the leaves and sprinkle with salt. Cover and cook over medium-high heat until all the spinach is wilted. Drain in a colander and press with a large spoon to remove as much water as possible.

2. Lay the veal flat and trim the excess fat (do not remove all of it, or the roast will be too dry when done). Spread the spinach over the veal and add the garlic cloves evenly spaced apart. Roll up the veal jelly-roll fashion and tie it securely with kitchen twine.

3. Put the butter and vegetable oil in a heavy braising pan that will hold the veal comfortably and place it over high heat. When the oil and butter are hot, put in the veal and brown it well on all sides. Season with salt and pepper, then add the wine. Allow the wine to bubble for 1 to 2 minutes to evaporate the alcohol and use a wooden spoon to loosen the tasty bits stuck to

the bottom of the pan. Add the tomatoes. When they begin to bubble, lower the heat so that the contents of the pan cook at a gentle but steady simmer. Cover the pan with the lid slightly askew and cook until the meat is tender when pierced with a fork, about 1½ to 2 hours. Turn the meat from time to time and add a little water to the pan if all the liquid evaporates before the veal is done.

4. When ready to serve, cut the veal in slices about ½ inch thick and remove the twine. If the sauce in the pan needs to be reduced, raise the heat and cook until it is thick enough to coat a spoon. Arrange the veal slices on a platter and pour the hot sauce over them. Serve at once.

NOTE: The veal can be prepared and cooked a day or even two ahead of time. When you are ready to serve, slice it and reheat the slices in the sauce over low heat.

SERVES 4 TO 6 PEOPLE

Sweet-and-Sour Braised Veal Shanks

OSSOBUCO IN AGRODOLCE

This is a different approach to the usual ossobuco with tomatoes and vegetables. It is cooked with vinegar and raisins, whose sweet and sour flavors, I find, complement the richness of veal shanks splendidly. It also has fewer ingredients than the traditional recipe and is less time-consuming to prepare.

25 *minutes to prepare*

2 ½ *hours from start to finish*

¼ cup golden raisins

2 cups yellow onion, very thinly sliced crosswise

3 tablespoons extra-virgin olive oil

Salt

2 to 3 tablespoons vegetable oil

About ½ cup all-purpose flour (enough to coat the veal)

Four 1½-inch-thick pieces veal shank

Freshly ground black pepper

¼ cup red wine vinegar

1 small beef bouillon cube

1 tablespoon shredded fresh basil leaves

½ teaspoon chopped fresh thyme leaves

1 teaspoon grated lemon zest

1. Place the raisins in a small bowl and cover with water.

2. Put the onion and olive oil in a heavy braising pan large enough to accommodate the veal shanks in a single layer. Place it over medium heat and sprinkle the onion lightly with salt. Cook until the onion turns a light caramel color. It may be necessary to raise the heat at the end to get the onion to color.

3. While the onion is cooking, put enough vegetable oil in a large skillet to come about ¼ inch up the sides and place it over high heat. Put the flour on a plate, roll the veal shanks in it, and shake off the excess. When the oil is hot, carefully slip in the meat and brown it on both sides. Transfer to a platter and season with salt and pepper.

4. Once the onion is colored, raise the heat to medium-high. Add the vinegar and let it bubble for about 30 seconds. Put in the browned veal shanks. Add enough water to come halfway

up the shanks and add the bouillon cube. Add the basil, thyme, and lemon zest. Lift the raisins out of the soaking water, squeeze out the excess water, and add them to the pan. Cover and cook at a moderate but steady simmer until the meat is very tender, about 2 hours. While they are cooking, turn the veal shanks occasionally. Add more water if all the liquid evaporates before they are done. If the sauce is too watery at the end, remove the meat, raise the heat, and reduce it until it is thick enough to coat a spoon. Serve hot.

N O T E : This is one of those dishes that actually improves after a day or two. Reheat the veal in its sauce over moderate heat, adding a little water if necessary.

SERVES 4 PEOPLE

Calf's Liver with Raisins and Onions

FEGATO IN SAOR

This dish is a combination of two Venetian recipes: *fegato alla veneziana* and *sfogi in saor*. The former is the well-known sautéed liver with onions, and the latter is fried sole in a sweet-and-sour marinade. I confess I am not a big fan of liver, but my wife is and she loves the recipe. The sweetness of the onions and raisins together with the red wine vinegar complement liver beautifully.

35-40 *minutes from start to finish*

½ cup golden raisins
4 cups yellow onion, very thinly sliced
    crosswise
3 tablespoons extra-virgin olive oil
Salt
Freshly ground black pepper

3 tablespoons red wine vinegar
3 tablespoons pine nuts
2 tablespoons vegetable oil
1½ pounds calf's liver, sliced ¼ inch thick
About ½ cup all-purpose flour (enough
    to coat the liver)

1. Put the raisins in a bowl and cover with water.

2. Put the onion and olive oil in a large skillet and place it over medium heat. Season the onion with salt and pepper and cook until the onion wilts completely and turns a light caramel color. It may be necessary to raise the heat at the end to color the onion.

3. When the onion is done, add the vinegar. Lift the raisins out of the soaking water, squeeze out the excess water, and add them to the pan along with the pine nuts. Stir well and cook for about 1 minute. Remove the pan from the heat and set aside.

4. Put the vegetable oil in a clean large skillet and place it over high heat. When the oil is hot, coat the liver with the flour, shake off the excess, and carefully slip the slices into the pan. Cook very briefly, about 1 minute on each side, then season with salt and pepper. Place the pan with the onions over medium-low heat and add the cooked liver. Turn each slice in the onions so that it is well coated and serve at once.

NOTE: The onion can easily be prepared several hours ahead of time. Make sure you reheat it before starting to cook the liver.

SERVES 4 TO 6 PEOPLE

Sautéed Pork Chops with Grapes

COSTOLETTE DI MAIALE ALL'UVA

The sweetness of grapes complements the savoriness of pork perfectly in this recipe. I prefer using thinly sliced pork chops because they can cook faster and at a higher heat to create a tasty crust.

minutes from start to finish **15**

2 tablespoons butter

1 tablespoon vegetable oil

1½ pounds thin pork chops (about ½ inch thick)

8 ounces green seedless grapes (about 1½ cups)

Salt

Freshly ground black pepper

2 tablespoons grappa or brandy

¼ cup Concord grape juice

1. Put 1 tablespoon of the butter and the vegetable oil in a skillet large enough to accommodate the pork chops and place it over medium-high heat. When the butter and oil are hot enough to make the meat sizzle, slide in the chops and cook for about 3 minutes on each side.

2. While the pork is cooking, rinse the grapes and cut them in half.

3. Remove the chops from the pan and season them with salt and pepper. Reduce the heat to medium and add the grappa to the pan. Make sure to keep your face away from the pan, because the steam from the grappa can be very hot. When the alcohol is mostly evaporated, 10 to 15 seconds, add the grape juice and grapes, season with a little salt, and loosen any tasty bits from the bottom of the pan with a wooden spoon. Check to see if the pork is completely cooked by making a small cut in one of the chops. If it is too pink, return the chops to the pan and let them continue to cook as the grape juice cooks down. If the chops do not need any more cooking time, leave them aside and reduce the sauce so that it is thick enough to coat a spoon. Swirl in the remaining 1 tablespoon butter and turn the pork chops in the sauce to coat them well. Serve at once.

SERVES 4 PEOPLE

Pork Chops with Fresh Fennel
COSTOLETTE DI MAIALE AL FINOCCHIO

Fennel is a wonderfully versatile vegetable. When eaten raw, it has a refreshing licorice flavor and is excellent in salads. Cooked, it becomes delicate and sweet and, in this dish, perfectly complements the savoriness of pork.

30 *minutes from start to finish*

2 fennel bulbs
1 tablespoon vegetable oil
1 tablespoon butter
8 pork loin chops (no thicker than
    ½ inch)

Salt
Freshly ground black pepper
2 tablespoons red wine vinegar

1. Cut away the tops of the fennel bulbs. Slice them lengthwise in half, then crosswise very thinly into half-rings. Soak the fennel slices in a bowl of cold water.

2. Put the oil and butter in a sauté pan large enough to hold all the chops snugly in a single layer and place it over high heat. When the oil is hot, carefully slide in half the pork chops. Brown them well on both sides, then transfer them to a platter. Repeat with the remaining chops. (Browning the chops in batches rather than trying to crowd all of them at once guarantees a crisp brown crust.) Season the pork with salt and pepper.

3. Add the vinegar to the pan and let it bubble for a few seconds while loosening the tasty bits on the bottom of the pan with a wooden spoon. Drain the fennel and add it to the pan. Season with salt and pepper, add a few tablespoons water, and cover the pan. Cook for about 5 minutes. Return the chops to the pan, cover, and continue cooking until the pork is quite tender, about 20 minutes. If there is still liquid in the pan when the chops are done, remove them and raise the heat to evaporate the liquid. The fennel should be almost creamy in consistency. Turn the chops in the fennel to coat them and serve at once.

SERVES 4 PEOPLE

Pork Loin Braised with Savoy Cabbage

ARROSTO DI MAIALE ALLA VERZA

In this recipe the Savoy cabbage cooks along with the pork until it becomes so creamy and tender that it becomes a sauce for the meat. I use red wine here to give the dish a robust flavor. If you prefer a more delicate flavor, use a dry white wine instead.

minutes to prepare **20**

hours from start to finish **2 ⅓**

6 cups shredded Savoy cabbage
2½ tablespoons butter
Salt
Freshly ground black pepper
1 tablespoon vegetable oil

2 pounds boneless pork loin,
    preferably center-cut
¼ cup dry, full-bodied red wine
2 bay leaves

1. Choose a heavy braising pan that will comfortably hold the pork. Put in the shredded cabbage and 1½ tablespoons of the butter and place the pan over medium heat. Season with salt and pepper and add about ½ cup water. Cover the pan and cook until the cabbage is wilted, about 10 minutes. Transfer the cabbage and any liquid in the pan to a bowl and set aside.

2. Put the remaining 1 tablespoon butter and the vegetable oil in the pan and raise the heat to high. When the oil and butter are hot, put in the pork loin. It will probably fit more easily and cook better if you cut it in half. Brown the meat on all sides, then season it with salt and pepper. Add the wine and let the alcohol bubble away while loosening the tasty bits that are stuck to the bottom of the pan with a wooden spoon. Put the cabbage with its liquid back in the pan, add the bay leaves, adjust the heat to a moderate but steady simmer, and put the cover on askew. Cook until the meat is tender, about 2 hours. Turn the pork occasionally while it is cooking, and if all the liquid evaporates before it is done, add a little water.

3. When the meat is done, take it out of the pan and cut it into thin slices, about ¼ inch thick. Raise the heat under the pan and cook the sauce until it thickens a bit. Or, if it is too

dry, add a little water. Return the pork to the pan and turn the slices to coat them with the sauce. Serve hot.

N O T E : As with most braised meats, this dish can be prepared up to a day in advance. When you are ready to serve, slice the meat, reheat the sauce, and heat the pork in the sauce for 2 to 3 minutes.

SERVES 6 PEOPLE

Beans and Sausage

SALSICCE E FAGIOLI

Beans and sausage is an inspired combination. The delicate creaminess of cooked beans (which should not be al dente, as most restaurants now seem to be serving them) complements the savory chunkiness of pork sausage perfectly. When I tested this recipe in the middle of a steamy Florida summer, I thoroughly enjoyed a dish that I had previously thought of only as winter comfort food. I recommend using plain, fresh pork sausage without fennel seeds.

minutes from start to finish (if using canned beans) **25**

1½ cans (15 ounces each) cannellini beans, drained, or 9 ounces dried beans
2 tablespoons extra-virgin olive oil
3 garlic cloves, lightly crushed and peeled

1 tablespoon fresh sage leaves
1¼ cups canned whole peeled tomatoes with their juice, coarsely chopped
Salt
Freshly ground black pepper
1 pound pork sausage links

1. If you are using dried beans, the day before, put them in a bowl and cover with cold water. Let them soak overnight. The next day, bring about 4 quarts water to a boil in a pot—*do not add salt*, or the skins of the beans will become tough—and cook the beans until tender, about 25 to 30 minutes.

2. Put the olive oil and garlic in a heavy saucepan that will hold the sausages in a single layer. Place it over medium-high heat and sauté the garlic cloves until lightly browned on all sides.

3. While the garlic is browning, coarsely chop the fresh sage. When the garlic has browned, discard it. Add the sage to the pan and cook, stirring, for about 1 minute. Add the tomatoes and beans. Season with salt and pepper, keeping in mind that the sausages are already fairly salty.

4. Add the sausage. When the tomatoes begin to bubble, turn the heat down to medium-low. Cover the pan and cook at a gentle simmer until the sausages feel tender when pricked with a fork, about 20 minutes. Check the pan occasionally and add a little water if all the liquid

evaporates before the sausages are done. Do not be concerned if some of the beans become mashed during the cooking. It only adds to the lusciousness of the dish. Serve hot.

N O T E : This dish can easily be prepared ahead of time and will keep for several days in the refrigerator. Reheat over gentle heat, adding 1 to 2 tablespoons water if the consistency has become too thick.

SERVES 4 TO 6 PEOPLE

Grilled Lamb Chops with a Lemon and Vinegar Sauce

COSTOLETTE DI AGNELLO SAPORITE

For a variation on plain grilled lamb chops, try serving them with this tangy, fresh-tasting sauce. The vinegar and lemon balance lamb's distinctive rich flavor, making this a preparation that may please even those who do not usually like lamb.

minutes from start to finish **25**

1 tablespoon finely chopped Italian flat-leaf parsley

1 teaspoon finely chopped garlic

2 tablespoons freshly squeezed lemon juice

2 tablespoons red wine vinegar

Salt

4 tablespoons extra-virgin olive oil

8 lamb loin chops (at least 1 inch thick), or 12 rib chops

Freshly ground black pepper

1. Light the grill.

2. While the grill is heating, prepare the sauce. Chop the parsley and garlic and mix them with the lemon juice, vinegar, and ½ teaspoon salt. Add the olive oil and stir well.

3. When the grill is very hot, cook the lamb chops, seasoning them with salt and pepper after turning them. When they are medium-rare or cooked to your desired degree of doneness, transfer them to a platter, pour the sauce over the chops, and serve at once.

SERVES 4 PEOPLE

Rack of Lamb Encrusted
with Parmesan Cheese

COSTOLETTE DI AGNELLO AL FORNO

This elegant and delectable rack of lamb is extremely simple to prepare. Tender and juicy lamb is surrounded by a crispy and tasty crust of Parmesan cheese and bread crumbs.

10 *minutes to prepare*

45 *minutes from start to finish*

2 Frenched racks of lamb (approximately 3 pounds)
1 tablespoon extra-virgin olive oil
Salt
Freshly ground black pepper

1 teaspoon finely chopped fresh rosemary leaves, or ½ teaspoon dried
2 tablespoons freshly grated Parmigiano-Reggiano
1 tablespoon plain fine dry bread crumbs

1. Preheat the oven to 400°F.

2. Place the racks of lamb in a baking pan, pour the olive oil over them, and spread it over the lamb with your fingers or a basting brush. Season with salt and pepper, then sprinkle with the rosemary.

3. Put the lamb in the upper level of the preheated oven and bake for 35 minutes for medium-rare. (Cook it 5 minutes less for rare or 5 minutes more for medium.)

4. Mix the Parmigiano-Reggiano and bread crumbs together on a plate large enough to accommodate the racks of lamb.

5. When you have taken the meat out of the oven, raise the heat to 450°F. Grasp one lamb rack by the ribs with a pot holder, place it on the bread crumb and cheese mixture, and turn to coat it on all sides. Put the lamb back in the baking pan and repeat with the second rack. Sprinkle any remaining bread crumb and cheese mixture over the racks. Return the pan to the oven and bake for another 5 minutes.

6. Take the lamb out of the oven, cut the racks into individual chops, and serve at once.

SERVES 4 PEOPLE

Lamb Shoulder Braised with Tomatoes

FRICCÒ DI AGNELLO ALLA CERNAIA

I had this delectable lamb dish at a restaurant called La Taverna del Lupo in Gubbio, a town about twenty miles north of Assisi. The meat cooks slowly with herbs and tomatoes and becomes so moist and tender it almost melts in your mouth.

minutes to prepare **15**
minutes from start to finish **90**

2 tablespoons extra-virgin olive oil
3 pounds bone-in lamb shoulder, cut
    into slices 1 to 1½ inches thick
Salt
Freshly ground black pepper
1 teaspoon fresh sage leaves

1 teaspoon fresh rosemary leaves
2 teaspoons finely chopped garlic
½ cup dry white wine
1½ cups canned whole peeled tomatoes
    with their juice, coarsely chopped
2 bay leaves

1. Heat the olive oil over high heat in a heavy braising pan that can accommodate the lamb snugly. When the oil is hot, brown half the lamb on both sides. Transfer it to a platter and repeat with the remaining lamb. Season with salt and pepper and remove the pan from the heat.

2. Chop the sage and rosemary and add to the pan along with the chopped garlic. Stir a few times, and return the pan to high heat. As soon as the herbs start to sizzle, add the white wine. Let it reduce a little so that the alcohol evaporates, then add the tomatoes and bay leaves. Season lightly with salt and pepper. Put the lamb back in the pan, reduce the heat so that the liquid is bubbling at a gentle but steady simmer, and place the cover on the pan slightly askew. Cook, turning the meat every 15 to 20 minutes, until it becomes very tender, 1 to 1½ hours. If the liquid in the pan evaporates before the meat is done, add a little water.

3. Transfer the lamb to a platter. If there is still too much liquid in the pan, raise the heat to reduce the sauce. Skim off any excess fat, pour the sauce over the meat, and serve.

NOTE: This dish is just as good 1 or 2 days after it is made. To reheat, add 2 tablespoons water, cover the pan, and place it over medium-low heat for 10 to 15 minutes.

SERVES 4 TO 6 PEOPLE

the pot and cook until the meat is tender when pierced with a fork, about 1¾ hours. Stir the contents of the pot occasionally, and if all the liquid evaporates before the meat is done, add a little water.

3. When the meat is tender, add the cannellini beans and cook covered for another 15 minutes. Serve at once.

NOTE: Like most stews, this dish can easily be made 1 or 2 days ahead. If you are making it ahead, wait to add the beans until you are ready to serve it and reheat over gentle heat.

SERVES 4 TO 6 PEOPLE

Savory Three-Meat Loaf with Simple Tomato Sauce

POLPETTONE SAPORITO

Using three different kinds of meat gives this simple meat loaf a distinctive flavor. I like to serve it with the simple tomato sauce recipe from my first book, *The Classic Pasta Cookbook,* that is given below.

30 *minutes to prepare*

80 *minutes from start to finish*

2 tablespoons butter
1 cup finely chopped yellow onion
½ cup finely diced celery
3 slices white bread
¼ cup hearty, dry red wine
8 ounces ground beef
8 ounces ground veal
8 ounces ground pork
1 teaspoon fresh marjoram leaves
1 teaspoon fresh oregano leaves
½ teaspoon fresh thyme leaves

1 large egg
Salt
Freshly ground black pepper

For the Sauce:
2 cups canned whole peeled tomatoes with their juice, coarsely chopped
4 tablespoons butter
1 small yellow onion, peeled and cut in half
Salt

1. Preheat the oven to 350°F.

2. Melt the butter in a small skillet over medium-high heat. Add the chopped onion and sauté until it turns a rich golden color.

3. While the onion is sautéing, dice the celery. Remove the crusts from the bread, chop the bread into small pieces, and set aside. When the onion is ready, add the celery and continue sautéing until it begins to color. Add the red wine and let it bubble for about 30 seconds to let the alcohol evaporate. Add the chopped bread, stir a few times, then remove from the heat.

4. In a bowl, mix the 3 ground meats with the freshly chopped herbs. Lightly beat the egg and add it to the mixture. Add the contents of the skillet and season with salt and pepper. Mix very well, preferably with your hands, so that all the ingredients, especially the bread, are evenly distributed.

5. Transfer the mixture to an 8- to 9-inch loaf pan and place in the preheated oven. Bake for 1 hour.

6. While the meatloaf is baking, make the tomato sauce. Put the chopped tomatoes, butter, and onion in a saucepan over medium heat. Season with salt and cook until the sauce is reduced and no longer watery, 30 to 40 minutes. Remove it from the heat and discard the onion (or save it as a special treat for the cook).

7. Remove the meat loaf from the oven and unmold it by placing a plate upside down over the loaf pan and flipping it over. It is a good idea to do this over a sink and to tip it away from you, because hot juices may pour out. Cut into fairly thin slices, about ¼ inch thick, and serve with the tomato sauce, reheating it first if necessary.

SERVES 4 TO 6 PEOPLE

Meat Pie, "Pizza" Style

"PIZZA" DI CARNE

Here is a tasty, ingenious ground beef dish that looks and tastes like a pizza but has no dough. It has the traditional elements of an Italian *pizza Margherita:* tomatoes, mozzarella, and oregano. But here they provide the topping for a ground beef mixture. It is basically a round, flat meat loaf topped with pizza seasoning. This dish can be served as part of a buffet, as a hearty appetizer, or for a light lunch along with a salad.

15 *minutes to prepare*

35 *minutes from start to finish*

2 slices white bread
2 tablespoons whole milk
1 pound ground beef
½ cup freshly grated pecorino romano
2 tablespoons plain fine dry bread
    crumbs
2 large eggs
2 ounces pancetta, thinly sliced
Salt

Freshly ground black pepper
Butter for the baking dish
¾ cup drained canned whole peeled
    tomatoes, coarsely chopped
4 ounces fresh mozzarella
2 tablespoons shredded fresh basil
    leaves
½ teaspoon dried whole oregano leaves

1. Preheat the oven to 425°F.

2. Cut the crusts from the bread. Put the bread and milk in a small bowl and mash the bread with your hands to get a smooth paste. Transfer it to a large mixing bowl and add the beef, pecorino, bread crumbs, and eggs.

3. Chop the pancetta and add it to the bowl. Season lightly with salt and pepper. Mix everything together thoroughly with your hands.

4. Butter the bottom and sides of a pie dish approximately 10 inches in diameter. Put in the ground beef mixture and spread it out evenly with your hands. Cover with the tomatoes. Cut

the mozzarella into strips and arrange them over the tomatoes (I like creating the spokes of a wheel with them). Sprinkle the basil leaves on top along with the dried oregano.

5. Bake in the preheated oven for 20 minutes. Let the "pizza" settle for about 5 minutes after you take it out of the oven, then transfer it with 2 spatulas to a serving plate. Serve it hot or lukewarm.

SERVES 6 TO 8 PEOPLE

Vegetables

Sautéed Carrots with Parmesan Cheese

CAROTE AL BURRO E FORMAGGIO

Other than some peeling and cutting, all this dish requires is patience. Slow cooking and adding only a little water at a time concentrates and intensifies the flavor of these carrots, making them some of the most delectable sweet and tender carrots I have eaten.

40 *minutes from start to finish*

1½ pounds carrots	Freshly ground black pepper
4 tablespoons butter	¼ cup freshly grated Parmigiano-
Salt	Reggiano

1. Cut off the ends of the carrots and peel them. Cut them into sticks approximately ¼ inch thick and 1½ inches long.

2. Place the butter and carrots in a skillet that will accommodate the carrots no more than about two layers deep. Place over medium-high heat. When the butter has melted, season the carrots with salt and pepper, stir so that they are well coated, and then add about ¼ cup water. Cook uncovered, allowing the water to evaporate completely before adding more, about ¼ cup at a time, until the carrots are tender, 20 to 30 minutes.

3. While the carrots are cooking, grate the Parmigiano-Reggiano.

4. When the carrots are tender, raise the heat to high to allow the carrots to brown a little. Add the cheese, remove from the heat, and serve.

SERVES 4 TO 6 PEOPLE

Sautéed Carrots with Marsala

CAROTE AL MARSALA

This recipe is a variation on the previous one. Marsala is used here to accent the carrots' natural sweetness, which is contrasted nicely by adding some parsley.

minutes from start to finish 60

2 pounds carrots
4 tablespoons butter
Salt
Freshly ground black pepper

2 tablespoons finely chopped Italian flat-leaf parsley
⅓ cup dry Marsala
1 tablespoon all-purpose flour

1. Trim the ends of the carrots, peel them, and cut into rounds approximately ⅛ inch thick.

2. Place the butter and carrots in a skillet that will accommodate the carrots no more than about two layers deep. Place over medium-high heat. When the butter has melted, season the carrots with salt and pepper, stir so that they are well coated, and then add about ¼ cup water. Cook uncovered, allowing the water to evaporate completely before adding more, about ¼ cup at a time, until the carrots are tender, 20 to 30 minutes.

3. While the carrots are cooking, chop the parsley.

4. When the carrots are tender, reduce the heat to medium and sauté until they begin to brown and the edges begin to curl, another 15 to 20 minutes. Raise the heat and add the Marsala. Allow it to bubble away for about 30 seconds to evaporate the alcohol. Stir in the flour, then add the parsley. Cook for another 2 to 3 minutes and serve at once.

NOTE: These carrots may be prepared several hours ahead of time up to adding the Marsala. Leave them in the pan covered until you are ready to serve, then reheat them and make sure the pan is nice and hot before pouring in the Marsala.

SERVES 4 TO 6 PEOPLE

Grilled Portobello Mushrooms, Porcini Style

FUNGHI AI FERRI ALLA MODA DEI PORCINI

The following recipe is, in my opinion, one of the most delicious ways to prepare portobello mushrooms. It is my favorite of the many ways fresh porcini mushrooms are prepared in Italy. If you ever get the chance to sample fresh porcini mushrooms, you will be treated to one of the most luscious mushrooms I know. Occasionally I see them in specialty markets; they can be quite expensive but are definitely worth splurging for.

25 *minutes from start to finish*

1 pound portobello mushrooms, or fresh porcini, if available
2 teaspoons finely chopped garlic
2 tablespoons finely chopped Italian flat-leaf parsley
2 tablespoons extra-virgin olive oil
Salt
Freshly ground black pepper

1. Light the grill.

2. Separate the stems from the caps of the portobello mushrooms. Cut off the root ends of the stem and discard them. Slice the stems lengthwise about ¼ inch thick.

3. In a small bowl, mix the garlic, parsley, and olive oil together and season with salt and pepper. With a brush or a spoon, spread the mixture on both sides of the mushroom caps and the sliced stems, saving just a little of it for basting the mushrooms as they cook.

4. When the grill is hot, place the mushrooms caps gill side down and the sliced stems on the grill rack. After about 5 minutes, turn the pieces over and baste with the remaining parsley mixture. Cook until the mushrooms are tender, 5 to 6 more minutes. Serve at once.

SERVES 4 TO 6 PEOPLE

Zucchini Sautéed with Fresh Mint

ZUCCHINE ALLA MENTA

Mint gives these zucchini a refreshing flavor that makes them an excellent accompaniment for any hearty meat dish.

minutes from start to finish 20

1½ pounds small zucchini
2 tablespoons extra-virgin olive oil
1 teaspoon finely chopped garlic
1 tablespoon finely chopped Italian flat-
    leaf parsley

1 teaspoon fresh mint leaves
1 tablespoon fresh basil leaves
Salt
Freshly ground black pepper

1. Rinse the zucchini thoroughly under cold running water. (If there is a lot of dirt, soaking them in cold water for about 10 minutes will help loosen it.) Trim the ends, slice the zucchini lengthwise in half, and cut into wedges about ¼ inch thick and 1½ inches long.

2. Put the olive oil and garlic in a sauté pan large enough to hold the zucchini in a single layer and set it over medium high heat. As soon as the garlic begins to color, add the parsley and stir for about 30 seconds. Add the zucchini and cook, stirring occasionally, until the zucchini are tender, 8 to 10 minutes. It is best not to stir too often to allow the zucchini to brown lightly.

3. While the zucchini are cooking, coarsely chop the mint and finely shred the basil. When the zucchini are tender, season with salt and pepper and the fresh herbs. Stir for about 30 seconds, then remove from the heat and serve at once.

SERVES 4 TO 6 PEOPLE

Zucchini Sautéed with Onions and Tomatoes

ZUCCHINE AL POMODORO E CIPOLLE

One of the delicious memories I have of my grandmother Giulia's Friday night dinners is the sweet flavor of a dish of zucchini with tomatoes. This recipe is my re-creation of that wonderful taste memory.

45 minutes from start to finish

1 cup yellow onion, very thinly sliced
   crosswise
3 tablespoons extra-virgin olive oil
1½ pounds firm small zucchini
1 pound fresh, ripe plum tomatoes,
   coarsely chopped, or 1 cup canned

whole peeled tomatoes with their
   juice, coarsely chopped
Salt
Freshly ground black pepper

1. Put the onion and olive oil in a 10-inch skillet or sauté pan over medium-low heat. Sauté until the onion wilts and turns a light caramel color.

2. Rinse and scrub the zucchini. Trim the ends, slice them lengthwise in half, and cut into wedges no more than ¼ inch thick and 1 to 1½ inches long.

3. When the onion is done, add the zucchini and raise the heat to medium-high. Cook the zucchini until they begin to color lightly, stirring occasionally but not too often.

4. While the zucchini are cooking, peel (page 24) and seed the tomatoes if using fresh. Cut into julienne strips about ¼ inch thick.

5. Once the zucchini have colored a bit, add the tomatoes and season with salt and pepper. Cook until the liquid from the tomatoes is evaporated and the zucchini are tender. Serve at once.

SERVES 4 TO 6 PEOPLE

Mrs. Torti's Zucchini

LE ZUCCHINE DELLA SIGNORA TORTI

This is a recipe I put together from childhood memories of a dish that a friend of my mother's used to make. I remember it because I was amazed at how tasty her zucchini were. Ideally this would be made with zucchini no thicker than ¾ inch and cooked whole. If you cannot find zucchini that small, choose the smallest available and cut them in half.

minutes from start to finish 35-40

⅔ cup finely chopped yellow onion
4 tablespoons extra-virgin olive oil
1 tablespoon finely chopped garlic
1½ pounds small zucchini
Salt
Freshly ground black pepper

1 teaspoon chopped fresh oregano
  leaves
2 tablespoons red wine vinegar
5 or 6 anchovy fillets, chopped
2 tablespoons finely chopped Italian
  flat-leaf parsley

1. Put the onion and olive oil in a skillet large enough to accommodate all the zucchini in a single layer. Place it over medium-low heat. Sauté until the onion turns a light caramel color.

2. While the onion is sautéing, chop the garlic. Rinse the zucchini and trim the ends. If the zucchini are thicker than ¾ inch, cut them lengthwise in half.

3. When the onion is done, raise the heat to medium-high, put in the garlic, and sauté for about 1 minute. Place the zucchini in the pan in a single layer. Season with salt and pepper. Add the oregano and vinegar. Allow the vinegar to bubble for about 30 seconds, then cover the pan and cook until the zucchini become tender, 10 to 15 minutes. Turn the zucchini after about 5 minutes so that they will color lightly on both sides.

4. When the zucchini are done, transfer them to a serving platter. Add the anchovies to the pan and stir with a wooden spoon until they begin to dissolve. Raise the heat and add about ¼ cup water and the parsley. Cook until the sauce is thick enough to coat the spoon, then pour it over the zucchini. Serve at once or at room temperature, but do not reheat the zucchini.

SERVES 4 PEOPLE

Zucchini Stuffed with Ground Beef and Mozzarella

ZUCCHINE RIPIENE

This dish is satisfying as a single-course meal and ideal for a buffet. I like it both hot and at room temperature. It is a great way to use those large zucchini one gets in the summer.

20 *minutes to prepare*

60 *minutes from start to finish*

Salt

1½ pounds medium to large zucchini, rinsed

½ cup finely chopped yellow onion

4 teaspoons finely chopped Italian flat-leaf parsley

6 ounces ground beef chuck

1 large egg

2 tablespoons fine dry bread crumbs, plus a little more for topping

Freshly ground black pepper

8 ounces fresh whole-milk mozzarella

Extra-virgin olive oil for drizzling

1. Preheat the oven to 375°F.

2. Fill a pot large enough to hold the zucchini with water and bring it to a boil. Add about 2 tablespoons salt and slide in the zucchini. Boil until tender when pricked with a fork, 8 to 10 minutes.

3. While the zucchini are cooking, chop the onion and parsley and place them in a mixing bowl. Add the ground beef, egg, and bread crumbs. Season with salt and pepper and mix well.

4. When the zucchini are cooked, remove them from the boiling water and cut them lengthwise in half. If the zucchini are too hot to handle, let them cool after you have cut them in half. Using a spoon or a small melon baller, scoop out the insides of the zucchini halves. (You can save the pulp and use it to make a delicious frittata.)

5. Sprinkle the zucchini cavities with a little salt and put them in a baking dish. Cut the mozzarella into very thin slices, line the zucchini cavities with them, and then fill with the ground beef mixture. Sprinkle some bread crumbs on top and drizzle with a little olive oil.

6. Place in the preheated oven and bake for 30 minutes. If the tops are still not lightly browned, place the dish under the broiler for 2 to 3 minutes. Allow to settle for a few minutes before serving warm, or serve at room temperature.

SERVES 4 TO 6 PEOPLE

Potatoes Stewed with Onions and Tomatoes

PATATE STUFATE

This is the perfect comfort food for cold dreary days when good food seems to be the best antidote. This dish would be a great accompaniment to grilled or roasted meats or *bollito misto,* moist and tender mixed boiled meats. Leftovers can be turned into a wonderful soup by adding some broth.

15–20 *minutes to prepare*

45 *minutes from start to finish*

1½ pounds yellow onions, sliced length-
    wise about ⅛ inch thick
3 tablespoons extra-virgin olive oil
Salt

1½ pounds boiling potatoes
1 pound fresh, ripe tomatoes
Freshly ground black pepper

1. Put the onions and olive oil in a 4- to 6-quart braising pot and place it over medium heat. Season lightly with salt and cook until the onions wilt completely and turn a pale golden color.

2. While the onions are cooking, peel the potatoes and cut them into ¾-inch cubes. Place them in a bowl with cold water to prevent them from turning brown. Peel the tomatoes (page 24) and chop them.

3. When the onions are ready, drain the potatoes and add them to the onions along with the tomatoes. Season with salt and generously with pepper. Add about ¼ cup water and cover the pot. Cook, stirring occasionally, until the potatoes are tender, 20 to 30 minutes. If all the liquid evaporates before the potatoes are done, add a little more water. Serve hot.

SERVES 4 TO 6 PEOPLE

Porcini Mashed Potatoes

PURÉ DI PATATE AI PORCINI

Here is a very easy way to dress up mashed potatoes. Combined with dried porcini, they become a very elegant and flavorful side dish.

minutes to prepare 10

minutes from start to finish 40

1 ounce dried porcini mushrooms
1 pound boiling potatoes
2 tablespoons butter
3 to 4 garlic cloves, lightly crushed and
    peeled

Salt
Freshly ground black pepper
½ cup whole milk

1. Put the dried porcini in a small bowl, cover with water, and soak until softened, about 15 minutes.

2. Peel the potatoes, put them in a pot, and cover them with water. Place the pot over medium-high heat and cook until tender, about 30 minutes, depending on the size of the potatoes, then remove them from the pot.

3. When the porcini are softened, lift them out of the water and squeeze the excess water back into the bowl. Filter the water through a paper towel or coffee filter. Rinse the mushrooms under running water and coarsely chop them.

4. Put the butter and garlic cloves in a small skillet over medium-high heat and lightly brown the garlic. Add the chopped porcini and the soaking water. Season with salt and pepper, raise the heat, and cook until almost all the liquid is evaporated.

5. Put the milk in a small saucepan over medium heat and heat until it is steaming hot but not boiling. Keeping an eye on the milk, purée the potatoes through a food mill or potato ricer. Remove the garlic cloves from the porcini and stir the porcini into the potatoes. When the milk is hot, add it to the potatoes a little at a time while beating the potatoes with a fork. Taste for salt and serve at once.

SERVES 4 TO 6 PEOPLE

Artichoke and Potato Casserole
CARCIOFI E PATATE AL FORNO

Potatoes have the wonderful ability to absorb flavors. In this dish they become infused with the flavor of artichokes. You can serve this as part of a buffet or dinner or as a vegetarian main dish.

25 *minutes to prepare*

60 *minutes from start to finish*

3 medium artichokes

2 lemons

1¼ pounds medium boiling potatoes, such as Yukon Gold, or small white potatoes

2 tablespoons extra-virgin olive oil, plus more if needed

Salt

Freshly ground black pepper

1 teaspoon finely chopped garlic

1 tablespoon finely chopped Italian flat-leaf parsley

½ cup freshly grated pecorino romano

1 tablespoon plain fine dry bread crumbs

1. Preheat the oven to 400°F.

2. Trim the artichokes, following the instructions on page 28 and using 1 of the lemons for rubbing the cut surfaces. Cut them in half lengthwise and then into very thin lengthwise slices and put them in a bowl with enough cold water to cover, mixed with the juice of the remaining lemon.

3. Peel the potatoes and slice them no more than ⅛ inch thick. Slicing them on a mandoline is the easiest and fastest way to do this. Put the slices in a bowl with enough cold water to cover to prevent them from becoming brown.

4. Lightly coat the bottom of an 8- by 10-inch baking dish with a little of the olive oil and spread one-third of the potato slices over the bottom of the dish. Season lightly with salt and pepper. Sprinkle a little of the garlic, parsley, and grated cheese over the potatoes, then drizzle some olive oil on top. Layer half of the artichoke slices over the potatoes, season with salt

and pepper, and top with a little more garlic, parsley, grated cheese, and olive oil. Continue layering and seasoning the potatoes and artichokes, ending with the last layer of potatoes. Pour about ⅓ cup water into the dish, sprinkle the bread crumbs over the top, and cover the dish with aluminum foil.

5. Bake in the preheated oven until the vegetables are tender when pricked with a fork, about 30 minutes. Remove the foil, raise the oven temperature to 450°F, and bake until the top layer becomes lightly browned, another 5 to 10 minutes. Allow the dish to settle for about 5 minutes before serving.

SERVES 4 TO 6 PEOPLE

Green Beans with Fresh Tomatoes and Ham

FAGIOLINI IN UMIDO

This is a hearty vegetable dish that is great on its own with some rice or as an accompaniment to most meat dishes. If you like spicy dishes, substitute crushed red pepper flakes for the black pepper.

45 *minutes from start to finish*

1½ cups yellow onion, thinly sliced crosswise

1½ tablespoons butter

Salt

3 ounces boiled ham, sliced ¼ inch thick

1 pound fresh, ripe tomatoes, peeled and diced (page 24)

1 pound green beans, ends trimmed and rinsed

Freshly ground black pepper

1. Put the onion and butter in a sauté pan large enough to accommodate the green beans and place it over medium heat. Season lightly with salt to help the onion wilt, and cook until it turns a golden color.

2. While the onion is cooking, cut the ham slices into strips ⅛ inch thick and 1 inch long. You should also have time to begin peeling and dicing the tomatoes and snapping off the ends of the green beans and rinsing them.

3. When the onion is ready, add the ham and cook until the strips begin to brown. Add the tomatoes and beans. Season with a little salt and several grindings of black pepper. Add about ¼ cup water and cover the pan. Cook until the beans are tender, 20 to 25 minutes. Stir occasionally, and if all the liquid evaporates before they are done, add a little more water. Serve hot.

SERVES 4 TO 6 PEOPLE

Tuscan Beans with Tomatoes and Rosemary

FAGIOLI AL POMODORO

Beans are an innately Tuscan food. To deprive a Tuscan of beans is to take away an essential nourishment of both body and soul. The ideal bean to use here is the cranberry bean, available fresh in the spring. The raw beans (as well as the pod) are white with red spots, but once cooked, they turn a reddish brown color. When fresh beans are not available, canned beans are an excellent substitute. A more economical alternative, which requires a bit more work, is using dried beans.

minutes from start to finish if using fresh beans **50**

minutes from start to finish if using canned beans **20**

4 tablespoons extra-virgin olive oil
4 garlic cloves, lightly crushed and peeled
3 branches fresh rosemary
2 cups canned whole peeled tomatoes
  with their juice, coarsely chopped
34 ounces canned cranberry beans (sometimes called Roman beans or *borlotti*)
  or cannellini beans, drained, or 4½

pounds fresh beans in the pod, shelled
and cooked in unsalted boiling water
until tender (25 to 30 minutes), or 13
ounces dried beans, soaked overnight
and cooked in unsalted boiling water
until tender (25 to 30 minutes)
Salt
Freshly ground black pepper

1. Put the olive oil, garlic, and rosemary in a 3- to 4-quart heavy saucepan over medium-high heat. Lightly brown the garlic on all sides, then remove the garlic and rosemary and discard.

2. Add the canned tomatoes to the pan. When they begin to bubble, adjust the heat so that they are cooking at a moderate simmer. Cook, stirring occasionally, for about 10 minutes.

3. Add the beans, season with salt and pepper, and cook until the tomatoes are no longer watery, about 5 more minutes. Serve hot.

N O T E : The beans can easily be prepared ahead of time and will keep in the refrigerator for several days. When reheating them, it may be necessary to add a little water.

SERVES 6 PEOPLE AS A SIDE DISH OR 3 PEOPLE AS A MAIN DISH

Gratinéed Fennel with Parmesan Cheese

FINOCCHI ALLA PARMIGIANA

Fennel, or anise, as it is sometimes called, has a distinct licorice flavor when raw and adds a fresh, bright taste to salads. When it is cooked, however, it transforms into a sweet and delicate vegetable. As with all white vegetables, it will be sweeter if you do not salt the water it is boiled in and season it only after it is cooked.

30 *minutes from start to finish*

3 large or 4 to 5 small fennel bulbs	3 tablespoons butter
Salt	¼ cup freshly grated Parmigiano-
Freshly ground black pepper	Reggiano

1. Bring a large pot of water to a boil.

2. Cut off the fennel tops where they meet the bulb and discard them. Pare any bruised or brownish parts from each bulb and remove a thin slice from the bottom. Slice the bulbs lengthwise about ¼ inch thick and soak them in a bowl of cold water.

3. Preheat the oven to 450°F.

4. Drain the fennel and slip it into the boiling water. Cook until tender, 5 to 10 minutes. Lift the fennel out of the water carefully so as not to break the slices (some will inevitably break but you can still use them).

5. In one or more shallow baking dishes or cookie sheets, arrange the fennel in a single layer. Season with salt and pepper, dot with the butter, and sprinkle with the Parmigiano-Reggiano. Bake in the preheated oven until golden brown, 10 to 15 minutes. Remove from the oven and serve at once.

SERVES 6 PEOPLE

Gratinéed Red, Green, and Yellow Peppers

PEPERONI GRATINATI

This is a very easy side dish that goes particularly well with grilled meats or roasted chicken. The tartness of the green peppers contrasts nicely with the sweetness of the red and yellow peppers.

minutes to prepare **10**

minutes from start to finish **30-35**

1 red bell pepper

1 yellow bell pepper

1 green bell pepper

2 tablespoons finely chopped Italian flat-
    leaf parsley

1 teaspoon finely chopped garlic

3 tablespoons extra-virgin olive oil

2 tablespoons plain fine dry bread
    crumbs

Salt

Freshly ground black pepper

1. Preheat the oven to 450°F.

2. Cut the peppers along the grooves into 3 or 4 pieces each, peel them with a vegetable peeler (page 26) and remove the seeds and core. Put them in a baking dish in which they fit in a single layer. Add the parsley, garlic, olive oil, and bread crumbs and season with salt and pepper. Toss well until all the ingredients are evenly distributed.

3. Place the dish in the upper third of the preheated oven and bake until the peppers are tender, about 15 minutes. Turn on the broiler and broil for 3 to 4 minutes to brown the tops of the peppers a little. Remove from the broiler and allow to cool for about 5 minutes before serving, or the peppers will be too hot to eat.

SERVES 4 PEOPLE

Cauliflower Gratin with Tomato and Fresh Sheep's Milk Cheese

CAVOLFIORE AL FORNO CON PRIMOSALE

Primosale, which translates literally as "first salt," is a fresh sheep's milk cheese typical of southern Italy. It is occasionally available in the States, but you can substitute any young, white sheep's milk cheese that is firm enough to slice. You can serve this as a side dish, part of a buffet, or a vegetarian main course.

45 *minutes from start to finish*

1 large head cauliflower (about 2 pounds)
¼ cup finely chopped yellow onion
3 tablespoons butter
2 cups canned whole peeled tomatoes
    with their juice, coarsely chopped
¾ cup freshly grated Parmigiano-
    Reggiano

Salt
Freshly ground black pepper
6 ounces sheep's milk cheese
    (see note above)

1. Place a pot of water large enough to accommodate the cauliflower over high heat and bring to a boil.

2. Preheat the oven to 375°F.

3. Quarter the cauliflower and discard all the leaves. When the water comes to a boil, put in the cauliflower (do not add salt) and cook until tender, about 20 minutes.

4. While the cauliflower is cooking, put the onion and 2 tablespoons of the butter in a 9- or 10-inch skillet over medium-low heat. Sauté the onion until it turns a light caramel color. Add the tomatoes and cook until the tomatoes are no longer watery and the butter begins to rise to the surface, 15 to 20 minutes. Transfer the tomato sauce to a large mixing bowl and stir in the Parmigiano-Reggiano.

5. When the cauliflower is cooked, drain it, cut it into bite-size pieces, and add it to the tomato sauce. Season with salt and pepper and toss gently until it is well coated with the sauce.

6. Choose a baking dish that will accommodate the cauliflower in two layers, approximately 8 by 11 inches. Put half of the cauliflower in the dish. Cut the sheep's milk cheese into very thin slices, using a sharp knife or a cheese slicer, and sprinkle half over the cauliflower. Put in the remaining cauliflower and tomato sauce and add the remaining cheese. Dot with the remaining 1 tablespoon butter.

7. Place the dish in the preheated oven and bake until the cheese melts, about 15 minutes. Serve hot or lukewarm.

SERVES 4 TO 6 PEOPLE

Oven-Roasted Vegetables
VERDURE AL FORNO

I love the taste of these vegetables, because oven-roasting them intensifies their flavor. They are the perfect accompaniment to almost any meat or fish course, but they are also wonderful all by themselves.

40 *minutes from start to finish*

2 pounds small red potatoes
1½ pounds yellow onions
2 large red or yellow bell peppers
1 green bell pepper
6 garlic cloves, lightly crushed and
   peeled

2 teaspoons chopped fresh rosemary
   leaves, or 1 teaspoon dried
Salt
Freshly ground black pepper
⅓ cup extra-virgin olive oil

1. Preheat the oven to 400°F.

2. Scrub the potatoes and cut them into ¾-inch chunks. Place them in a bowl of cold water so they will not turn brown.

3. Cut the onions in half, peel them, and cut into 1-inch-thick wedges.

4. Peel the peppers (page 26), remove the cores and seeds, and cut into 1-inch squares.

5. Drain the potatoes and combine them with the onions and peppers in a baking pan large enough to accommodate them in a snug single layer. Add the garlic cloves and rosemary. Season with salt and pepper, add the olive oil, and toss until all the vegetables are well coated.

6. Place the baking pan in the upper third of the preheated oven. Bake for about 30 minutes, turning the vegetables over with a spoon every 10 minutes. The dish is done when the vegetables are tender and the edges are browned. If the vegetables are tender but have not browned, raise the heat to 450°F and bake for another 5 minutes. Allow the dish to rest for about 5 minutes before serving.

SERVES 4 TO 6 PEOPLE

Spinach Loaf
TORTA DI SPINACI

Here is a dish that is ideally suited for a buffet when served at room temperature. When served warm, it is an elegant side dish, yet it is substantial enough to be served as a vegetarian entrée.

minutes to prepare 30
minutes from start to finish 75

2 pounds fresh spinach
Salt
4 large eggs
1 cup whole milk
1 tablespoon all-purpose flour
⅓ cup freshly grated Parmigiano-Reggiano

Pinch of freshly grated nutmeg
Butter for the loaf pan
About 3 tablespoons plain fine dry bread crumbs

1. Rinse the spinach well and remove any thick, tough stems. Put the spinach in a pot with about ½ cup water and sprinkle with salt. Place over medium-high heat and cover the pot. Cook until tender, about 10 minutes. Pour the spinach into a colander and let it drain.

2. Preheat the oven to 350°F.

3. Beat the eggs with the milk in a mixing bowl, then mix in the flour. Stir in the Parmigiano-Reggiano and nutmeg. Press the spinach against the sides of the colander with the back of a large serving spoon to squeeze out the excess water. Transfer the spinach to a cutting board and coarsely chop it. Add it to the egg mixture and mix well.

4. Butter the bottom and sides of a 9-inch loaf pan. Put in about 2 tablespoons of the bread crumbs and shake the pan around to coat the buttered sides and bottom. Pour in the spinach mixture and top with the remaining bread crumbs.

5. Bake in the preheated oven until the top begins to brown, about 45 minutes. Remove the loaf from the oven and unmold it onto a flat serving platter. Slice the loaf about ½ inch thick and serve either warm or at room temperature.

SERVES 4 TO 6 PEOPLE

Tricolor Vegetable Casserole

TEGLIA MULTICOLORE

This colorful vegetarian casserole is perfect for a buffet or a satisfying vegetarian meal.

25 *minutes to prepare*

60 *minutes from start to finish*

1 red bell pepper
⅓ cup finely chopped yellow onion
2 tablespoons butter, plus more for the
  baking dish
½ cup whole milk
2 tablespoons all-purpose flour
5 large eggs

½ cup freshly grated Parmigiano-
  Reggiano
Salt
Freshly ground black pepper
1½ cups frozen tiny peas (about
  9 ounces), thawed

1. Roast the pepper whole until the skin is charred on all sides. You can do this on a barbecue grill, over the open flame of a gas burner, or under the broiler. When the pepper is done, put it in a plastic bag and tie a knot to seal it. The steam trapped in the bag will make it very easy to remove the skin later.

2. Preheat the oven to 400°F.

3. Put the onion and butter in a medium skillet over medium heat. Sauté until the onion turns a light caramel color.

4. While the onion is sautéing, combine the milk, flour, eggs, and Parmigiano-Reggiano in a mixing bowl. Season with salt and pepper and mix well with a whisk or fork.

5. When the onion is ready, add the peas and raise the heat to medium-high. Season with salt and pepper and sauté for about 5 minutes.

6. While the peas are sautéing, take the pepper out of the bag and remove the skin. Cut the pepper open and remove the core, seeds, and white pith. Cut it into long, thin strips.

7. Mix the sautéed peas and onion into the egg mixture along with most of the roasted pepper strips, keeping back a few to decorate the top of the casserole.

8. Butter the bottom and sides of a baking dish approximately 7 to 8 inches in diameter and 3 inches deep. Pour in the vegetable mixture and top with the remaining strips of roasted pepper. Place in the preheated oven and bake until the mixture is firm and the top has browned lightly, about 35 minutes. Serve lukewarm or hot.

SERVES 4 TO 6 PEOPLE

Salads

Mixed Green Salad

INSALATA MISTA

At the end of the meal, just before fruit or dessert is served, Italians often eat a salad. It may be composed of many different lettuces and raw vegetables or simply one very fresh, tender lettuce. The dressing usually consists of three ingredients: salt, a very good extra-virgin olive oil, and red wine vinegar. A well-known Italian proverb says it takes four people to dress a salad: a wise person to add the salt, a generous person for the olive oil, a stingy person for the vinegar, and a patient person to toss (my father always told me a salad must be tossed thirty-four times). On special occasions, I add a fifth person to this team: a wealthy person for the balsamic vinegar. In the following recipe, I provide precise measurements, but I would encourage you not to measure. The vegetables here are simply suggestions and can be changed according to the season or one's desire. For example, you could add fresh tomatoes when they are sweet and flavorful in the summer, or contrast a sweet-tasting lettuce with a spicy green like arugula or frisée. The combinations need only be limited by your imagination and what you find at the market.

15 *minutes from start to finish*

1 large or 2 small heads of your favorite lettuce(s)	Salt
	5 tablespoons extra-virgin olive oil
1 red or yellow bell pepper, or ½ of each	2 teaspoons red wine vinegar
1 medium carrot	1 teaspoon balsamic vinegar

1. Tear the lettuce leaves into bite-size pieces and rinse in cold water. Dry the leaves, using a salad spinner or by wrapping a clean dry towel around them and shaking it over the sink. Transfer to a salad bowl.

2. Rinse the pepper, remove the core and seeds, and cut it into strips about ¼ inch wide and 1½ inches long. Add it to the lettuce.

3. Peel the carrot and grate it, using the larger holes of your grater, into the salad bowl.

4. Season with salt, add the olive oil and both vinegars, and toss well. Serve at once.

SERVES 4 TO 6 PEOPLE

Crunchy Salad

INSALATA CROCCANTE

This is a refreshing combination of fruit and vegetables. The sweetness of the apple perfectly balances the slight bitterness of the radicchio and endive. All the ingredients have a wonderfully satisfying crunch to them.

minutes from start to finish **15–20**

2 cups julienned celery sticks, about ⅛ inch thick and 1 to 1½ inches long
1 carrot
1 medium head radicchio
1 medium head Belgian endive

1 small Granny Smith apple
3 tablespoons freshly squeezed lemon juice
Salt
5 tablespoons extra-virgin olive oil

1. Cut the celery, using the heart and innermost stalks, which are the most tender, first. Place it in a salad bowl.

2. Peel the carrot and grate it, using the larger holes of a grater, into the salad bowl.

3. Discard any bruised or wilted leaves from the radicchio. Rinse and dry the remaining leaves and tear them into bite-size pieces. Trim the heart and put it in the salad bowl along with the leaves. Do the same with the Belgian endive.

4. Peel the apple, remove the core, and cut into sticks slightly smaller than the celery. Toss the pieces in a small bowl with 1 tablespoon of the lemon juice before adding them to the rest of the ingredients. (The salad can be prepared up to this point 2 hours ahead of time. It is not necessary to refrigerate it.)

5. When you are ready to serve, season the salad with salt, the olive oil, and the remaining 2 tablespoons lemon juice. Toss well and taste to see if it needs any more seasoning. Serve at once.

SERVES 4 TO 6 PEOPLE

Mushroom, Arugula, and Parmesan Salad

INSALATA DI FUNGHI, RUCOLA, E PARMIGIANO

Mushroom and Parmesan salad is often found in Italy in the fall, when it is made with *ovuli,* a wild mushroom that is excellent raw. When using the milder cultivated mushrooms, I have found the peppery taste of arugula adds a richness of flavor that makes up for the absence of *ovuli.* Now that a wide variety of wild mushrooms is available in some markets, you may want to experiment with some and omit the arugula. This dish is excellent as an appetizer or a more substantial salad at the end of a meal.

15 *minutes from start to finish*

6 ounces arugula
8 ounces firm cremini or white
    mushrooms
Salt
5 tablespoons extra-virgin olive oil

1 tablespoon freshly squeezed lemon
    juice
Freshly ground black pepper
½ cup Parmigiano-Reggiano shavings,
    cut with a vegetable peeler

1. Remove the stems from the arugula and rinse the leaves in several changes of cold water.

2. Wipe the mushrooms clean with a damp paper towel and trim the stems if bruised. Very thinly slice the mushrooms lengthwise.

3. In a salad bowl, combine the mushrooms and arugula. Season with salt, the olive oil, lemon juice, and pepper. Toss until the arugula and mushrooms are well coated with the dressing. Transfer the salad to individual salad plates and top with the Parmigiano-Reggiano shavings.

SERVES 4 TO 6 PEOPLE

Tomato, Mozzarella, and Basil Salad

INSALATA CAPRESE

Ideally this salad would be made with just-picked Neapolitan tomatoes, fresh buffalo milk mozzarella, and newly pressed, premium extra-virgin olive oil. With summer garden tomatoes at their peak, buffalo milk mozzarella just flown in from Italy, and one of the many wonderful olive oils now available, you can get pretty close. However, even without those elusive ingredients, the combination of reasonably flavorful tomatoes, cow's milk mozzarella, fresh basil, and an excellent olive oil is an inspired mélange of flavors.

minutes from start to finish IO

1 to 2 choice vine-ripened tomatoes
 (about 12 ounces)
8 ounces whole-milk mozzarella, preferably buffalo milk
16 fresh basil leaves

About 2 teaspoons extra-virgin olive oil
Salt
Freshly ground black pepper

1. Cut the tomatoes and mozzarella into ¼-inch-thick slices.

2. Arrange the salad on individual serving plates, placing 4 tomato slices, 4 mozzarella slices, and 4 basil leaves on each plate in loosely overlapping rows.

3. Just before serving, pour a thin stream of olive oil over each plate and season with salt and plenty of black pepper.

SERVES 4 PEOPLE

Summer Salad with Baked Red Onions

INSALATA DI CIPOLLE AL FORNO

This hearty salad combines the richness of baked red onion with the freshness of ripe raw tomatoes. The dressing is a savory vinaigrette with capers and anchovies. It is an ideal dish for a buffet or, with the addition of some good canned tuna, for a light lunch or picnic.

15 *minutes to prepare*

90 *minutes from start to finish*

2 medium red onions, unpeeled
4 large eggs
8 ounces vine-ripened tomatoes
6 anchovy fillets
1 tablespoon capers

4 teaspoons red wine vinegar
Small pinch of salt
5 tablespoons extra-virgin olive oil
8 ounces premium canned tuna packed
   in olive oil (optional)

1. Preheat the oven to 400°F.

2. Put the unpeeled onions on a baking sheet and bake until the onions feel tender when pinched, about 1 hour. Remove from the oven and allow to cool.

3. Put the eggs and enough water to cover in a pot and place it over high heat. When the water begins to boil, reduce the heat to a simmer and cook the eggs for 10 minutes or less, depending on how dry you like the yolk. Place the pot under cold running water to cool the eggs and stop the cooking.

4. Peel the onions and cut into 1-inch chunks. Place them in a salad bowl.

5. Cut the tomatoes into wedges and add them to the onions.

6. Put the anchovies, capers, vinegar, and salt in a food processor and pulse until almost creamy. Add the olive oil and run the processor just long enough to blend it into the dressing.

7. Peel the hard-boiled eggs, cut them into wedges, and add to the salad bowl.

8. Pour the dressing over the salad and toss gently. If adding the tuna, drain it and toss with the salad. Serve at room temperature.

SERVES 4 TO 6 PEOPLE

Marinated Green Beans
FAGIOLINI MARINATI

This fragrant salad is perfect for a summer buffet or picnic. The beans are tossed with all the other ingredients while they are still hot, which allows them to absorb as much of the flavors as possible. Adding the vinegar to the beans when they are hot causes some of the acidity from the vinegar to evaporate while maintaining all its richness of flavor.

25 *minutes from start to finish*

1½ pounds green beans
Salt
12 large green olives
4 garlic cloves
3 tablespoons finely shredded fresh basil
    leaves

1 tablespoon coarsely chopped fresh
    oregano leaves
1 tablespoon capers
1½ tablespoons red wine vinegar
5 tablespoons extra-virgin olive oil

1. Fill a pot large enough to hold the green beans with water, place over high heat, and bring to a boil.

2. While the water is heating, snap off the ends of the beans and rinse them in cold water. When the water comes to a boil, salt it generously (about 1 teaspoon per quart of water) and put in the beans. Cook until they are tender all the way through but not mushy, 8 to 10 minutes.

3. While the beans are cooking, sliver the olives by slicing the flesh away from the pits. Lightly crush and peel the garlic cloves, shred the basil, and coarsely chop the oregano. Put the olives, garlic, basil, oregano, and capers in the salad bowl you will be using.

4. When the beans are cooked, drain them well and add them to the salad bowl. Add the vinegar and toss. Add the olive oil, toss again, and taste for salt. Let stand at room temperature for about 3 hours and remove the garlic cloves before serving.

NOTE: This salad can be made a day ahead and kept covered in the refrigerator. Be sure to let it come to room temperature before serving.

SERVES 4 TO 6 PEOPLE

Red Cabbage Slaw
INSALATA DI CAVOLO NERO

When I presented this salad to my wife, Lael, she exclaimed, "Oh, you made coleslaw?" "Try it anyway," I said. "Hmm, it doesn't taste like coleslaw. It's good though." So here it is, *Italian* coleslaw!

minutes from start to finish **15–20**

12 ounces red cabbage

1 sweet onion, such as Vidalia, Walla Walla, or Florida Sweet

10 green olives, slivered by slicing the flesh away from the pits

Salt

6 tablespoons extra-virgin olive oil

2 tablespoons red wine vinegar

1. Shred the cabbage approximately ⅛ inch thick and place it in a salad bowl. Very thinly slice the onion crosswise. If it is not mild enough, soak it in several changes of cold water for 10 to 15 minutes. Add it to the cabbage along with the olives.

2. Dress the salad with salt, the olive oil, and red wine vinegar and serve right away.

SERVES 6 TO 8 PEOPLE

Tuna and Italian Rice Salad

INSALATA DI RISO E TONNO

This colorful and tasty rice salad is a perfect summer dish to bring along on a picnic or set out on a buffet table. I use an Italian risotto rice, such as Arborio or Carnaroli. I like the chewy texture, and I find its inherent starchiness perfect for absorbing all the different flavors of the salad.

30 *minutes from start to finish*

Salt

1 cup rice for risotto, such as Arborio or Carnaroli

2 eggs

1 red bell pepper

16 Kalamata olives

4 ounces premium canned tuna packed in olive oil (½ cup drained)

½ cup capers

4 tablespoons extra-virgin olive oil

1 tablespoon red wine vinegar

1. Fill a pot with at least 1 quart water and bring it to a boil. Add about 1 teaspoon salt and pour in the rice. Cover the pot and cook the rice at a moderate boil until it is al dente, about 20 minutes, stirring occasionally to prevent it from sticking. When it is done, drain the rice and rinse it under cold water.

2. While the rice is cooking, cook the eggs in simmering water until hard-boiled, about 10 minutes, then cool them under cold water and remove the shells. Cut the red pepper open and remove the core, seeds, and white pith. Cut the pepper into narrow strips about 1 inch long. Sliver the olives by cutting the flesh away from the pits.

3. Drain the tuna and place it in a large serving bowl. Cut the eggs into wedges and add them to the bowl. Add the red pepper, olives, capers, and cooked rice. Add the olive oil and vinegar, season with salt, and toss well. Serve at room temperature.

NOTE: You can make the salad a day ahead and refrigerate it covered. Be sure to let it come to room temperature before you serve it.

SERVES 4 TO 6 PEOPLE

Tomato, Basil, and Bread Salad
PANE E POMODORO

At the end of an exquisite meal of many courses at Aimo e Nadia, one of Milan's finest restaurants, the chef/owner, Aimo, insisted my wife and I try some "bread and tomatoes." Our stomachs were bursting, but after the first bite it was impossible not to finish every morsel of the generous portion he had brought us. The bread cubes were steeped with the fresh, sweet flavor of tomato, and the dish was a delicious and refreshing end to our meal.

The flavor of this dish is totally dependent on the quality of the ingredients. Use only the best extra-virgin olive oil and vine-ripened tomatoes.

minutes to prepare 15
minutes from start to finish 75

3 cups ¾-inch cubes white Italian or
    French bread, without the crust
1½ pounds fresh, ripe, sweet tomatoes

12 to 16 fresh basil leaves
Salt
3 tablespoons extra-virgin olive oil

1. Place the bread cubes in a serving bowl.

2. Peel the tomatoes (page 24), and remove the seeds. Put the tomatoes in a food processor and chop to a very fine consistency, almost a purée. The yield should be about 1½ cups. Pour the tomatoes over the bread in the serving bowl.

3. Cut the basil leaves into strips and add to the bowl. Season with salt and add the olive oil. Toss well and let stand for about 1 hour before serving.

SERVES 4 TO 6 PEOPLE

Tomatoes, Green Beans, Yellow Peppers, and Tuna in a Mustard Dressing

INSALATA DI TONNO E FAGIOLINI

This is a colorful and refreshing salad that is substantial enough for a light lunch. As always, the quality of the ingredients is very important, and using a very good canned tuna packed in olive oil will make all the difference. I like to use yellow peppers because they make a nice contrast with the red of the tomatoes and they are also slightly sweeter, but a combination of red and yellow is fine, too, or if yellow peppers are not available, you can use only red.

20 *minutes from start to finish*

1½ pounds green beans
Salt
2 yellow bell peppers
1½ pounds firm, vine-ripened tomatoes
18 ounces premium canned tuna
    packed in olive oil

2 teaspoons Dijon mustard
2 tablespoons red wine vinegar
6 tablespoons extra-virgin olive oil
Freshly ground black pepper

1. Choose a pot that will hold the green beans, fill it with water, and place it over high heat.

2. Trim the string beans by snapping off both ends and rinse them in cold water. When the water comes to a boil, salt it generously (about 1 teaspoon per quart of water) and put in the beans. Cook until they are tender all the way through but not mushy, 8 to 10 minutes, depending on the size of the beans. Drain the beans well and put them in a salad bowl.

3. While the beans are cooking, remove the core, seeds, and white pith from the yellow peppers and cut the peppers into strips about 1 inch long and ¼ inch wide. Cut the tomatoes into wedges that are no more than ½ inch at their widest point. Drain the tuna and break it up into small bite-size pieces.

4. Put the tuna, tomatoes, and peppers in the salad bowl with the beans. Dissolve the mustard in the vinegar in a small bowl, stir in the olive oil, add some black pepper, and pour the mixture into the salad. Toss gently to combine. The salad can sit for about an hour, but do not add any salt until just before serving, as it will draw out water from the tomatoes and you may end up with a soup instead of a salad.

SERVES 6 PEOPLE

Chicken Salad with Pomegranate, Pine Nuts, and Raisins

INSALATA DI POLLO COL MELOGRANO

At a restaurant called Il Giardino in the town of San Lorenzo del Campo, on the central Italian Adriatic coast, I savored a capon salad in which the tanginess of pomegranate, the sweetness of pine nuts and raisins, and the saltiness of Parmigiano-Reggiano shavings created a symphony of contrasting flavors. The final touch was a dressing made with an olive oil from Cartoceto, a small medieval town about six miles inland known for producing outstanding oil. This recipe calls for chicken, but if you can make it with capon, it will give the dish a richer flavor.

35 *minutes from start to finish*

¼ cup raisins, preferably golden
1 pound boneless, skinless chicken breasts (see page 30 for boning instructions)
1 cup pomegranate seeds (from about 2 pomegranates), or ½ cup dried cranberries

¼ cup pine nuts
Salt
Freshly ground black pepper
6 tablespoons extra-virgin olive oil
¼ cup Parmigiano-Reggiano shavings, cut with a vegetable peeler

1. Soak the raisins (and cranberries if using) in enough cold water to cover in a bowl.

2. Fill a pot large enough to accommodate the chicken with water, and place it over high heat. When the water is boiling, put in the chicken and simmer for 10 to 15 minutes, depending on the thickness. To test for doneness, make a small cut in the thickest part of the breast. The flesh should be white and the juices should be clear. When the chicken is done, remove the pot from the heat and allow to cool. Keeping the chicken in the cooking water prevents it from drying out.

3. Slice the chicken into bite-size pieces and place them in the bowl you plan to serve the salad in. Lift the raisins (and cranberries if using) out of the water and gently squeeze them. Add them to the bowl along with the pomegranate seeds and pine nuts. Season with salt and pepper. Add the olive oil and toss until all the ingredients are well coated. Top with the Parmigiano-Reggiano shavings and serve.

SERVES 4 TO 6 PEOPLE

Desserts

Italian Apple Pie

TORTA DI MELE

Apple pie is not as uncommon a dessert in Italy as one might think, and this deep-dish version exemplifies the simplicity of Italian cooking. The only ingredients in the filling are apples, butter, and sugar. They are cooked slowly until their flavor is concentrated to what can best be described as "essence of apple," while still maintaining the texture of sliced apples.

25 *minutes to prepare*

2½ *hours from start to finish*

For the Filling:

About 1 tablespoon freshly squeezed
  lemon juice
3 pounds red apples, such as Fuji, Gala,
  or Rome Beauty
8 tablespoons (1 stick) unsalted butter
⅔ cup granulated sugar

For the Crust:

1⅓ cups all-purpose flour
⅓ cup granulated sugar
2 large egg yolks
6 tablespoons unsalted butter, cut into
  small pieces and brought to room
  temperature

1. For the filling, fill a bowl with cold water and add the lemon juice. Core and peel the apples. If you do not have an apple corer, use a stiff narrow knife to cut around the core at both ends, then push it out. Cut the apples lengthwise in half and thinly slice them crosswise. Put the cut apples in the bowl as you work to prevent them from turning brown.

2. Melt the butter in a 10-inch skillet over medium-low heat. When the butter begins to bubble, add the sugar. Drain the apple slices and add them to the skillet. Cook the apples, gently stirring them on occasion, until all the liquid they release evaporates and they begin to turn a very light caramel color. This will take about 1½ hours. The apples will become very tender, but their texture should not be that of applesauce, and most of the slices should retain their shape. Remove the skillet from the heat and allow the apples to cool in the pan until they are just lukewarm.

3. Preheat the oven to 350°F.

4. For the crust, put all the ingredients in a food processor and run the machine until they form a homogeneous mass. Remove it from the bowl and knead it with your hands until you get a smooth dough. Place it on a sheet of wax paper or aluminum foil and thin it out with a rolling pin until you form a circle that is about ⅛ inch thick and large enough to generously cover the top of a 9-inch pie dish.

5. Pour the cooked apples into the pie dish and press them down a bit with a spatula. Place the rolled-out dough on top and trim the overhang. Bake in the preheated oven until the crust turns golden brown, 15 to 20 minutes.

6. You can serve the pie from the dish or transfer it to a serving platter when the pie is slightly cooled and safe to handle but still warm. Invert it onto a cookie sheet and then again onto the serving platter so that it ends up with the crust on top. Serve at room temperature or chilled.

NOTE: The filling can be prepared a day ahead and kept covered in the refrigerator until you are ready to bake the pie. Add about 5 minutes to the baking time when using a cold filling.

SERVES 8 TO 10 PEOPLE

Sicilian Orange Tart

CROSTATA ALL'ARANCIA

I particularly like serving this tart at the end of a seafood meal because it is a wonderfully refreshing and aromatic dessert that leaves a clean taste in your mouth. It has received rave reviews whenever I have made it.

20 *minutes to prepare*

80 *minutes from start to finish*

For the Crust:
Grated zest of 2 oranges
2 cups all-purpose flour
½ cup granulated sugar
8 tablespoons (1 stick) unsalted butter,
    cut into about a dozen pieces
3 extra-large egg yolks
Pinch of salt
1 tablespoon ice water, or more if
    needed

For the Filling:
2 extra-large eggs
½ cup granulated sugar
¾ cup freshly squeezed orange juice
    (juice from the 2 grated oranges is
    usually sufficient)

1. Preheat the oven to 350°F.

2. For the crust, grate the orange zest using a light pressure on the grater so as not to dig into the white pith, which is bitter. Make the pastry shell by placing the flour, sugar, butter, egg yolks, orange zest, and salt in a food processor and running it until the ingredients are well mixed. Add the ice water and run the processor again until a dough is formed. If the mixture is too dry and does not hold together, add a little more ice water, 1 teaspoon at a time.

3. Remove the dough from the bowl of the processor (carefully taking out the blade first) and place it on the removable bottom of a shallow 11-inch tart pan. Using a rolling pin, roll out the dough until it is no more than ¼ inch thick, allowing the dough to extend over the edge. Slide the dough and tart pan bottom off the edge of the work surface, placing a hand under the

metal bottom, and lower it into the outer ring of the tart pan. Press the dough against the sides of the pan and trim the overhang.

4. Cover the dough with a sheet of aluminum foil and weight it with some rice or dried beans. Place the tart pan in the preheated oven and bake for 10 minutes. Remove the foil with the rice or beans and bake uncovered for another 10 minutes.

5. While the crust is baking, make the filling. Put the eggs and sugar in the bowl of a mixer. Beat at high speed until pale yellow ribbons form, 2 to 3 minutes. Reduce the speed of the mixer and slowly pour in the orange juice.

6. Pour the mixture into the baked crust and place the tart in the oven. Bake until the top is browned and the filling appears firm when the pan is shaken gently, about 40 minutes. Allow the tart to cool completely before serving. I prefer it after it has been chilled in the refrigerator.

SERVES 8 TO 10 PEOPLE

Almond Bread Pudding

BUDINO DI PANE ALLE MANDORLE

Do not let the length of the recipe dissuade you from trying this scrumptious bread pudding. I am not a cook who likes to spend time making desserts, but this one takes very little time to put together.

20 *minutes to prepare*

75 *minutes from start to finish*

5 tablespoons raisins
3 tablespoons good dark rum
About 12 ounces thinly sliced firm white bread (enough to line the bottom and sides and cover an 8- to 9-inch loaf pan)

4 tablespoons unsalted butter, softened
1 cup whole milk
4 extra-large eggs
7 tablespoons granulated sugar
3 ounces unblanched almonds (¾ cup)

1. Place the raisins in a small bowl with the rum and allow to soak.

2. Remove the crusts from the bread. Determine how much bread you will need by lining the sides, bottom, and top of an 8- to 9-inch loaf pan, trimming the slices of bread so that there are no gaps. Remove the bread from the loaf pan and use all the butter to coat both sides of the slices of bread. Line the sides and the bottom of the loaf pan with the buttered bread slices and set aside the slices that will go on top.

3. Pour the milk into a small saucepan and heat it over low heat until you see steam emerge when it is stirred. Do not let it come to a boil.

4. While the milk is heating and you are keeping a watchful eye on it, put the eggs and 4 tablespoons of the sugar in the bowl of a mixer. Beat at high speed until the mixture is pale yellow and forms ribbons when the beater is lifted, about 2 to 3 minutes.

5. With the mixer on low speed, slowly add the hot milk. When about half the milk has been incorporated, you can add the rest more quickly.

6. Place the almonds and remaining 3 tablespoons sugar in a food processor and pulse until they reach the consistency of coarsely ground black pepper. Mix the almond mixture into the custard.

7. Pour the custard into the bread-lined loaf pan, holding back about ½ cup. If the loaf pan fills to the top and you have more than ½ cup custard left, it is probably because it is too foamy. Just let it stand for a bit until it settles.

8. Take the raisins that have been soaking in the rum and distribute them over the custard in the loaf pan. Save the rum that is left over.

9. Preheat the oven to 325°F.

10. Cover the top of the filled loaf pan with the remaining buttered bread and pour the rest of the custard over the layer of bread. Let stand for about 15 minutes so that the bread becomes well soaked.

11. Place the bread pudding on the middle rack of the preheated oven and bake until it looks firm when the pan is jiggled, about 40 minutes. Remove it from the oven and allow it to cool for about 45 minutes to 1 hour.

12. Once the pudding is cool enough to handle, flip it over onto a flat serving platter. The pudding should unmold easily so that you can remove the loaf pan. Serve either chilled or at room temperature. Cut into ½-inch slices and sprinkle each serving with a few drops of the rum that was used to soak the raisins.

N O T E : This bread pudding can be made up to 5 days ahead and stored in the refrigerator.

SERVES 8 TO 10 PEOPLE

Apple and Pear Gratin

PASTICCIO DI MELE E PERE

This dessert is a rustic, delicious baked mixture of apple and pear slices in a custardlike base. It is also incredibly easy to make. Share it with family and friends in a casual setting.

15 minutes to prepare

60 minutes from start to finish

Butter for the baking dish
3 large eggs
2 large egg yolks
⅔ cup granulated sugar
1 tablespoon dark rum
½ teaspoon pure vanilla extract

2 tablespoons all-purpose flour
½ cup heavy cream
1 red apple, such as Fuji, Gala, or Rome Beauty
1 ripe Anjou or Bartlett pear

1. Preheat oven to 325°F. Butter the sides and bottom of a 9-inch baking dish that is at least 2 inches deep or a 9-inch springform pan.

2. Put the whole eggs plus the egg yolks and the sugar in the bowl of a mixer. Beat at high speed until you see pale yellow ribbons form.

3. Mix in the rum and vanilla. Add the flour and mix well. Transfer to a mixing bowl.

4. In the clean mixer bowl, whip the heavy cream to firm peaks, then fold it carefully into the egg mixture with a rubber spatula. Pour the batter into the buttered dish.

5. Peel and core the apple and pear and slice them crosswise into thin half-moons. Arrange over the batter in the baking dish, alternating the apple and pear slices. Do not be concerned if they sink into the mixture; they eventually will end up embedded in it. Place in the preheated oven and bake until the top has turned golden brown, 45 to 50 minutes. Serve warm or chilled.

SERVES 6 TO 8 PEOPLE

Chocolate Ricotta Pudding

CREMA DI RICOTTA AL CIOCCOLATO

It is not a mousse. It is not a custard. It is not really a pudding. It is a delicious, creamy chocolate dessert that is incredibly easy to make. It does have one drawback: It is rather addictive.

minutes to prepare, plus time for chilling **15**

8 ounces semisweet chocolate
6 large egg yolks
½ cup granulated sugar

¼ cup heavy cream
1½ cups whole-milk ricotta

1. Melt the chocolate in the top of a double boiler over simmering water. (You can create a makeshift double boiler by placing a metal bowl over a pot of water.)

2. While the chocolate is melting, put the egg yolks and sugar in the bowl of a mixer. Beat at high speed until the mixture is pale yellow and forms soft ribbons.

3. When the chocolate is melted, add the heavy cream and stir until it is completely blended. Pour the chocolate into the egg mixture and mix well. Add the ricotta and mix again until completely blended. Divide the mixture among 6 individual serving bowls or goblets. Refrigerate overnight before serving.

NOTE: If you are concerned about eating uncooked eggs, do not make this recipe. A dollop of freshly whipped cream over each serving makes for a wonderfully refreshing topping!

SERVES 6 PEOPLE

Chocolate and Amaretti Custard

CREMA DI CIOCCOLATA E AMARETTI

Here is a chocolate custard with an Italian twist: ground amaretti cookies. It makes for a rich and satisfying dessert that is easy to make and will keep for several days in the refrigerator.

20 *minutes to prepare, plus time for chilling*

4 cups whole milk
4 large egg yolks
½ cup granulated sugar
½ cup all-purpose flour

4 ounces amaretti cookies (10 pairs or 20 cookies of the Lazzaroni brand)
8 ounces semisweet chocolate

1. Put the milk in a saucepan and heat over medium heat until it is steaming when stirred but has not come to a boil. Remove it from the heat.

2. While the milk is heating, put the egg yolks and sugar in the bowl of a mixer. Beat at high speed until the mixture is pale yellow and forms soft ribbons. Add the flour and mix until it is completely blended. Transfer the milk to a pitcher and pour it into the mixing bowl very slowly while the mixer is running at low speed. After about one-third of the milk has been added and you can feel the mixing bowl warm up, you can pour the rest of the milk in at a faster rate. When all the milk has been mixed in, pour the mixture back into the saucepan and place it over medium-low heat. Cook, stirring with a whisk, until the custard thickens, about 10 minutes. Remove from the heat.

3. Put the amaretti in a food processor and finely chop. Coarsely chop the chocolate and add it to the amaretti in the food processor. Pulse the processor a few times so that the chocolate is uniformly chopped into small pieces.

4. Transfer the hot custard from the saucepan to a mixing bowl and stir in the amaretti mixture. The chocolate will melt and you should get a fairly smooth consistency. Pour the custard into individual goblets or dessert cups. Let it cool to room temperature, then cover with plastic wrap and chill in the refrigerator for at least 2 hours before serving.

NOTE: If you are concerned about eating uncooked eggs, do not make this recipe.

SERVES 6 TO 8 PEOPLE

Rum and Strawberry Layer Cake

DOLCE DI FRAGOLE

All you need to do to make this refreshing and light dessert is assemble the ingredients and chill.

minutes to prepare, plus time for chilling **20**

12 ounces fresh strawberries
1 cup confectioners' sugar
1 lemon
½ cup sweet white wine
12 Italian-style dry ladyfingers, also
    called *savoiardi* (about 4 ounces)

(if only the soft, moist kind is available, you can dry them in the oven at 250°F for 15 to 20 minutes)
2 tablespoons dark rum

1. Rinse the strawberries, remove the green tops, and cut them into bite-size pieces. Place them in a bowl with the confectioners' sugar. Gently grate the zest of the lemon, taking care not to dig into the white pith, and add it to the bowl. Juice the lemon and add the juice along with the wine to the strawberries. Toss well.

2. Choose a serving dish approximately 2 inches deep and 7 inches across and line the bottom with a layer of ladyfingers, breaking them into smaller pieces if necessary. Sprinkle half the rum over them, then put in all the strawberries, holding back as much of the juice as possible. Top with another layer of ladyfingers. Mix the remaining rum with the juice from the strawberries and pour it over the ladyfingers. Chill in the refrigerator for at least 3 hours, or even overnight, before serving.

SERVES 4 TO 6 PEOPLE

Tiramisù

There are probably as many variations of this sumptuous Venetian dessert as there are restaurants that serve it. This is my version, and it has elicited many moans of pleasure. One ingredient that is always used is mascarpone, a creamy, sweet, almost buttery cheese that is now available in most Italian specialty stores. The combination and type of liqueurs varies, but the classic liqueur for tiramisù is Strega. It is difficult to find and you can substitute yellow Chartreuse for it, but the unique flavor Strega gives this dessert makes it worth the effort to find it. The flavor of Italian coffee is essential here, but it is not necessary to use one of those expensive espresso machines to make good Italian coffee. Most Italians make their coffee in the morning with a stovetop Moka coffeemaker. It does the job very nicely and can be bought at a fraction of the cost. The bottom is filled with water, the filter is inserted and filled with coffee, and then the top is screwed on and the Moka placed on the stove over high heat. As the water heats, it turns to steam, which rises through the filter with the coffee and into the top part, where it condenses into liquid form again, and the coffee is done.

45 *minutes to prepare, plus time for chilling*

3 cups strong espresso coffee
4 large egg yolks
5 tablespoons granulated sugar
3 tablespoons Strega liqueur or yellow Chartreuse
2 tablespoons dark rum
1 container (500 grams) mascarpone cheese

⅓ cup heavy cream
8 ounces dry ladyfingers, also called *savoiardi* (if only the soft, moist kind is available, you can dry them in the oven at 250°F for 15 to 20 minutes)
About 1 tablespoon unsweetened cocoa

1. Make the coffee and pour it into a shallow bowl wide enough to use for soaking the ladyfingers. Set aside to cool.

2. Put the egg yolks and sugar in the bowl of a mixer. Beat at high speed until the mixture is pale yellow and forms soft ribbons.

3. Add the Strega and rum and continue mixing until well blended. Mix in the mascarpone, 3 to 4 tablespoons at a time, being careful not to overwhip it, or the mixture might break.

4. In a separate mixing bowl, whip the cream to firm peaks. Carefully fold it into the mascarpone mixture with a rubber spatula.

5. Soak the ladyfingers in the coffee, 1 or 2 at a time, allowing the liquid to penetrate them completely, and arrange half of them in a single layer in an 8- by 11-inch serving dish that is at least 1½ inches deep. Spread half of the mascarpone mixture over the ladyfingers. Cover with another layer of soaked ladyfingers and spread the remaining mascarpone mixture on top. Put the cocoa in a fine-mesh strainer or sifter and sprinkle over the top.

6. Cover the dish with plastic wrap and refrigerate for 24 hours, or at least overnight. When ready to serve, cut the tiramisù into square portions with a metal spatula and place them on flat dessert plates. For a nice finishing touch, sprinkle a little fresh cocoa on top before serving.

N O T E : If you are concerned about eating uncooked eggs, do not make this recipe.

SERVES 12 PEOPLE

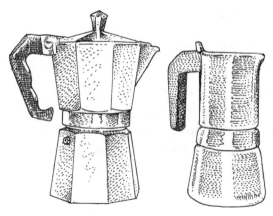

Moka coffeemakers

Pineapple Ice Cream

GELATO DI ANANAS

Homemade ice cream is always a big hit, and it's a dessert you can make ahead of time. It is not necessary to buy one of those expensive machines with a built-in freezer unless you are planning on regularly making several batches on the same day. An excellent result can be had even from modest ice-cream makers. When using those models with a cylinder that you have to freeze overnight, I have found that it is best to keep it in the freezer while you are making the ice cream as well.

IO–I5 *minutes to prepare*

30–40 *minutes from start to finish*

1 pound peeled and cored pineapple
¾ cup granulated sugar
1 cup cold water
½ cup heavy cream

1. Cut the pineapple into chunks and place it in a food processor with the sugar. Process until smooth. Add the water and process until it is well blended. Transfer to a mixing bowl.

2. In another mixing bowl, whip the cream with a whisk until it just begins to thicken. The consistency should resemble yogurt. Add it to the pineapple mixture in the bowl and mix well. Pour into an ice-cream maker and freeze following the manufacturer's instructions. When done, it will be rather soft but ready to eat just the same. If you prefer it firmer, put it in a container, cover well, and place in the freezer. After 2 to 3 hours, it will have hardened to normal ice-cream consistency.

NOTE: You can make cantaloupe ice cream by substituting cantaloupe for the pineapple and following the recipe exactly.

MAKES I QUART

Amaretto Cookie Frozen Dessert
SEMIFREDDO DI AMARETTI

A *semifreddo* is very much like ice cream except that you do not need an ice-cream machine to make it. Because the mixture contains beaten egg whites and whipped cream, there is enough air to prevent it from freezing too hard. You simply put it in the freezer, and it will not get any harder than the consistency of ice cream.

minutes to prepare, plus time for chilling **20**

2 large eggs
⅓ cup granulated sugar
6 ounces amaretti cookies (12 pairs or
    24 cookies of the Lazzaroni brand)

1 cup heavy cream
1 ounce unblanched almonds, coarsely
    chopped

1. Separate the eggs. Put the egg yolks and sugar in the bowl of a mixer. Beat at high speed until the mixture is pale yellow and forms soft ribbons.

2. Grind the amaretti cookies in a food processor until very fine, almost a powder. Add them to the egg yolk mixture and mix well with a rubber spatula.

3. Whip the egg whites until they form stiff peaks and fold them into the mixture. Whip the cream to firm peaks and fold it in as well.

4. Line an 8- to 9-inch loaf pan with wax paper. Sprinkle the chopped almonds on the bottom, then pour in the mixture. Freeze overnight.

5. When you are ready to serve, unmold the *semifreddo* onto a flat serving plate. To loosen it easily, wipe the bottom of the loaf pan with a sponge that has been soaked in hot water. Cut into ½-inch slices and serve.

NOTE: If you are concerned about eating uncooked eggs, do not make this recipe.

SERVES 8 PEOPLE

Coffee-Flavored Frozen Dessert with Warm Chocolate Sauce

SEMIFREDDO AL CAFFÉ

This dessert can be put together in a very short time and keeps well for several days. The flavor of Italian coffee is essential here, but it is not necessary to use one of those expensive espresso machines to make good Italian coffee. A stovetop Moka coffeemaker (see page 209) does the job very nicely and can be bought at a fraction of the cost. The chocolate sauce is also delicious for dipping fruit and can easily be reheated.

25 *minutes to prepare, plus time for chilling*

For the Semifreddo:
1¾ cups heavy cream
⅔ cup granulated sugar
⅔ cup strong espresso coffee, cooled
3 large eggs

For the Chocolate Sauce:
4 ounces semisweet chocolate
1 tablespoon unsalted butter
¼ cup heavy cream

1. For the *semifreddo,* whip the heavy cream and ⅓ cup of the sugar with an electric mixer to firm peaks. Add the cooled coffee and mix it in.

2. Separate the eggs. Place the egg yolks in a mixer bowl and add the remaining ⅓ cup sugar. Put 2 of the egg whites in a separate bowl and discard the third. Beat the egg yolks and sugar until the mixture is pale yellow and forms soft ribbons. Fold it into the whipped cream. Beat the 2 egg whites until they form stiff peaks and fold them into the mixture.

3. Line an 8- to 9-inch loaf pan with wax paper and pour in the mixture. Freeze overnight.

4. For the chocolate sauce, melt the chocolate with the butter in the top of a double boiler over simmering water. Remove from the heat and add the heavy cream and stir until smooth. The chocolate sauce can be made several hours ahead of time and kept at room temperature, or several days ahead and refrigerated.

5. When you are ready to serve, reheat the chocolate sauce gently in a double boiler. Unmold the *semifreddo* onto a flat serving plate. To loosen it easily, wipe the bottom of the loaf pan with a sponge that has been soaked in hot water. Cut the *semifreddo* into slices, place on dessert plates, pour a spoonful of chocolate sauce over each slice, and serve.

N O T E : If you are concerned about eating uncooked eggs, do not make this recipe.

SERVES 8 PEOPLE

Glazed Peaches in White Wine

PESCHE AL VINO

This extraordinarily simple dessert concentrates the flavor of peaches and perfumes them with lemon zest.

30 *minutes from start to finish*

2 tablespoons unsalted butter
4 ripe but firm peaches, peeled, halved, and pitted

1 lemon
¼ cup dry white wine
2 tablespoons granulated sugar

1. Put the butter in a skillet large enough to hold the peaches in a single layer and place it over medium-high heat. When the butter is hot and the foam begins to subside, slide in the peaches cut side down. Sauté until they just begin to brown, 2 to 3 minutes, then turn them over and sauté for another 2 to 3 minutes.

2. While the peaches are sautéing, remove the zest from the lemon with a sharp vegetable peeler, using a swivel sawing motion. Do not press down too hard, so as not to remove the white pith along with the zest, and try to end up with strips at least 2 inches long.

3. Once the peaches have sautéed on both sides, add the wine, sugar, and lemon zest. Cover the pan and cook over medium-low heat for about 20 minutes.

4. Transfer the peaches to a serving platter or individual plates and discard the lemon zest. The juice in the pan should have the consistency of syrup. If it is too thin, raise the heat and reduce it. Pour the syrup over the peaches. Serve lukewarm or at room temperature.

SERVES 4 PEOPLE

Mixed Fruit Marinated with Kirsch

FRUTTA MISTA AL KIRSCH

Kiwi and mango are hardly Italian fruits, but macerating fruit in liqueur is very Italian. If I were in Italy, I would use the wonderful sweet and aromatic peaches available there in the summer, but in the States, I have found that ripe mangoes most closely approximate that flavor. Kiwis, although not native to Italy, are becoming quite popular there, and I love the flavor and color they add to this dessert. Strawberries' sweetness complete the picture perfectly.

minutes to prepare, plus time for chilling **15**

2 ripe mangoes

1 pound fresh strawberries

2 ripe kiwis

2 tablespoons granulated sugar

⅓ cup freshly squeezed orange juice

2 tablespoons kirsch or other fruit brandy

1 medium lemon

1. Peel the mangoes, cut them into bite-size slices, and place in a shallow serving bowl.

2. Rinse the strawberries and cut off the green tops. Cut them lengthwise in halves or quarters, depending on the size, and add them to the mangoes.

3. Peel the kiwis, cut them lengthwise in half, and then slice crosswise into half-moons. Add them to the other fruit.

4. Add the sugar, orange juice, and kirsch to the fruit. Grate the zest of the lemon over the fruit, taking care not to dig into the white pith. Stir gently so that all the ingredients are well combined. Cover the bowl with plastic wrap and refrigerate for at least 2 hours, or even overnight, before serving.

SERVES 4 TO 6 PEOPLE

Lemon-Scented Almond Cookies

BISCOTTI ALLE MANDORLE

These low-fat cookies are ridiculously simple to make and absolutely delicious. For the first few days after they are made, they have a light crunch on the outside and are slightly chewy on the inside. By the fifth day (if you can wait that long to eat them), they become completely crisp. The Italian word *biscotti* refers to any cookie, not just the sliced, twice-baked cookies.

10 *minutes to prepare*

30 *minutes from start to finish*

8 ounces unblanched almonds (1½ cups)	2 large egg whites
¾ cup granulated sugar	Butter for the parchment paper or cookie sheet
¼ cup all-purpose flour	1 tablespoon confectioners' sugar, or more as needed
1 lemon	

1. Preheat the oven to 400°F.

2. Put the almonds and granulated sugar in a food processor and chop the almonds to a medium-coarse consistency. Transfer to a mixing bowl.

3. Add the flour and grate the lemon zest over the bowl, taking care not to dig into the white pith. Mix thoroughly. Add the egg whites and mix them in with a rubber spatula until a homogeneous but somewhat lumpy batter is formed.

4. Butter a sheet of parchment paper and place it on a cookie sheet or use a nonstick cookie sheet and butter it. Shape the cookies by filling a tablespoon (preferably round rather than oval) with batter. Place the cookies at least 1 inch apart on the cookie sheet.

5. Bake in the preheated oven until the cookies are very light brown in color, about 20 minutes. While they are still hot, dust the cookies with the confectioners' sugar, using a sifter or fine-mesh strainer. Let them cool completely, then remove from the parchment or cookie sheet, using a metal spatula.

MAKES APPROXIMATELY 28 COOKIES

Chocolate Puffs
CIUFFI DI CIOCCOLATO

You can impress your family and friends with these incredibly easy-to-make handmade chocolates.

minutes to prepare, plus time for chilling **25**

4 ounces golden raisins (about ½ cup)
12 ounces semisweet chocolate
4 ounces blanched hazelnuts
½ cup heavy cream

1. Put the raisins in a bowl with enough water to cover and soak until soft and plump, about 10 minutes.

2. Melt the chocolate. I find the easiest way to do this is in a double boiler over simmering water, but it can also be done in a 250°F oven or a microwave at medium power if you prefer.

3. Coarsely chop the hazelnuts either by hand or in a food processor.

4. Squeeze the excess water out of the raisins and add them to the melted chocolate along with the hazelnuts and cream. Mix with a spatula until completely blended. Line a cookie sheet with aluminum foil and use two spoons to place nuggets of the chocolate mixture on it. Refrigerate until the chocolates harden, about 1 hour. Serve chilled.

MAKES APPROXIMATELY 24 CHOCOLATES

Menus

A TRADITIONAL ITALIAN MEAL consists of several courses, none of which is considered the main course or entrée. The first course, or *primo,* is usually a pasta, a risotto, or a soup; this is followed by a meat, chicken, or fish dish, which is the *secondo,* or second course. The portion size and importance of the first and second courses is equal. Normally a vegetable, which is called *il contorno,* is served with the second course. The salad usually comes after the second course, because it refreshes and cleanses the palate. Desserts are served occasionally, but mostly reserved for special occasions. On most days, an Italian meal ends with fresh fruit, either as is or sliced and marinated, or with an assortment of cheeses.

I have divided this chapter into three parts. The first consists of simple menus: three-course menus for everyday meals. Since a full multicourse meal can be too much for every day, these menus feature either a *primo* or *secondo* rather than both. Elegant menus make up the next section. These follow the traditional format and are more involved four- or five-course meals for special occasions and entertaining. Then, I have put together three buffet menus, one based on fish, one based on meat, and a cold buffet. The chapter ends with two picnic menus because, after all, there is no reason why a meal outdoors should not be a special event with great food and excellent wine.

Naturally these are only suggestions, and I encourage you to try other combinations of recipes. The step-by-step directions for each menu reflect the way I would go about preparing the meal if I were doing it by myself. I have allowed plenty of time for each step; as you become more familiar with the recipes, you may be able to shorten the preparation times.

Simple Family Menus

SINCE THE ICE CREAM and the sauce for the fish are made ahead of time, this meal can be put together in about 20 minutes. I like having something refreshing after eating fish, but ripe seasonal fruit would also be a good way to end this meal.

Mushroom, Arugula, and Parmesan Salad (page 186)

Salmon Fillets with a Caper and Anchovy Sauce (page 94)

Pineapple Ice Cream (page 210)

45 *minutes to prepare*

1. Begin by sautéing the onion for the salmon. While the onion is cooking, make the ice cream. When the onion is ready, remove from the heat and set aside.

2. When you are ready to serve, rinse the arugula and clean the mushrooms for the salad. Put the onions back over medium heat, chop the parsley and anchovies, and proceed with step 3 of the salmon recipe.

3. While the fish is cooking, prepare the salad. Serve the fish with the salad but on separate plates.

THE SAUSAGE AND LEEK PASTA makes this a satisfying meal, while the appetizer and the fruit keep it light.

Tomato, Mozzarella, and Basil Salad (page 187)

Fusilli with Sausage and Leeks (page 72)

Mixed Fruit Marinated with Kirsch (page 215)

minutes to prepare 45

1. Prepare the fruit at least 2 hours before you are planning on serving it.

2. Make the sauce for the pasta but do not cook the pasta yet. While the leeks are cooking, put the water on for the pasta, prepare the salad, and grate the cheese for the pasta. When the leek sauce is done, remove it from the heat and set aside.

3. Serve the salad and start cooking the pasta. (It will take about 10 to 12 minutes for the pasta to cook.)

HERE IS A GREAT MENU for lunch or a light dinner. The peaches and the tuna can both be made several hours ahead of time so that the clam soup, which takes less than 25 minutes, is the only thing left to do when you are ready to serve.

Clam Soup with Fresh Tomatoes (page 61)

Fresh Tuna, Arugula, and Tomato (page 34)

Glazed Peaches in White Wine (page 214)

75 *minutes to prepare*

1. Make the peaches. While the peaches are cooking, prepare the tomatoes for the clam soup (step 1 of the recipe) and set them aside.

2. Assemble the fresh tuna, arugula, and tomato, without dressing it.

3. Make the clam soup, and serve it as soon as it is ready. After you have finished eating the soup, dress the tuna and serve. End the meal with the glazed peaches.

BOTH THE GREEN BEANS and the peaches need to be prepared ahead of time, so the pasta is the only thing that has to be done before serving. You could also do this menu with any of the other pasta recipes in this book.

Spaghetti with Tomatoes and Anchovies (page 65)

Marinated Green Beans (page 190)

Glazed Peaches in White Wine (page 214)

minutes to prepare, plus time for marinating 6O

1. At least 3 hours ahead of time, or the day before, prepare the green beans and the peaches. Begin with the peaches, and once you have added the wine and covered the pan, start the green beans. If serving them the same day, there is no need to put the green beans and the peaches in the refrigerator. If you make them the day before, refrigerate them, but remember to take them out at least 1 hour before serving.

2. About 30 minutes before serving, begin making the pasta dish. Serve the spaghetti first, then the string beans, and end with the peaches.

I LIKE SERVING THE TOMATO and bread salad after the pasta because it is so wonderfully refreshing after the richness of a carbonara sauce, but if you prefer, it can also be served as an appetizer. The dessert and the salad both have to be made ahead of time, so the pasta, which takes only 20 minutes, is the only thing that needs to be done before serving.

Spaghetti alla Carbonara with Zucchini (page 68)

Tomato, Basil, and Bread Salad (page 193)

Chocolate Ricotta Pudding (page 205)

50 *minutes to prepare*

1. Prepare the chocolate ricotta pudding 1 to 3 days before you plan on serving it.

2. Prepare the tomato and bread salad 1 to 3 hours before serving.

3. About 20 minutes before you plan on serving, begin making the pasta dish.

THIS CHICKEN DISH IS ONE OF MY FAVORITES. Its bold flavors go particularly well with the sweetness of baked fennel. The crunchy apple and radicchio salad gives a refreshing and palate-cleansing finish to the meal.

Chicken with Green Olives (page 120)

Gratinéed Fennel with Parmesan Cheese (page 174)

Crunchy Salad (page 185)

minutes to prepare 6o

1. Begin making the chicken. When the chicken is covered and cooking on its own, begin making the fennel dish.

2. As the fennel boils and then bakes, prepare the salad, but do not dress it until you are ready to serve it.

3. When everything is ready, serve the chicken and the fennel together. Afterward, dress the salad and serve it.

THE SWEET DELICATE FLAVOR of cooked fennel makes it an ideal accompaniment for this rustic, savory chicken dish. The time given is if you buy boneless chicken breasts, but boning the chicken breasts yourself will only add 5 to 10 minutes to the preparation time.

Chicken Breast Fillets with Red and Yellow Peppers (page 114)

Gratinéed Fennel with Parmesan Cheese (page 174)

Chocolate Ricotta Pudding (page 205)

60 *minutes to prepare, plus 15 minutes for the dessert the day before*

1. Make the chocolate ricotta pudding the day before.

2. Begin preparing the fennel, but wait to turn on the oven. Once the fennel is in the boiling water, start the chicken recipe. Take out the fennel when it is tender and lay the slices out in a shallow baking dish. Just before adding the tomatoes to the chicken sauce, turn on the oven. When the sauce for the chicken is done, put the fennel in the oven.

3. After you have deglazed the pan for the chicken and put the vegetables back in it, remove the pan from the heat and wait for the fennel to be done before continuing. Once the fennel is out of the oven, place the pan with the vegetables over medium heat, put the chicken back in, and let it heat through, about 1 minute. Serve the chicken with the fennel. End with the chocolate ricotta pudding.

THE GRILL IS RAPIDLY BECOMING one of the most popular cooking appliances. You can cook almost anything on a grill: meats, fish, vegetables, and even fruit. It gives food a wonderful flavor and is usually a very quick and simple way to prepare a meal.

Grilled Lamb Chops with a Lemon and Vinegar Sauce (page 141)

Grilled Portobello Mushrooms, Porcini Style (page 162)

Mixed Green Salad (page 184)

minutes to prepare 35

1. Prepare the salad, but do not dress it until you are ready to serve it.

2. Light the grill. While you wait for it to get hot, trim and slice the portobello mushrooms as directed in step 2 of the recipe. Chop the garlic and parsley for both the mushrooms and the sauce for the lamb. Make the marinade for the mushrooms and brush them with it. Make the sauce for the lamb and set it aside.

3. When the grill is hot, put on the lamb chops and the mushrooms. The mushrooms will probably be done before the lamb. Remove them from the grill and keep them on a warm plate while the lamb chops finish cooking.

4. Serve the lamb chops with the mushrooms and follow with the salad afterward.

ALTHOUGH THE PREPARATION TIME may seem long, everything in this menu can be made ahead of time and requires minimal attention. The pork and the bread pudding can be made 1 to 2 days ahead, and the carrots can be left in the pan (before adding the cheese) for several hours.

Pork Loin Braised with Savoy Cabbage (page 137)

Sautéed Carrots with Parmesan Cheese (page 160)

Almond Bread Pudding (page 202)

105 *minutes to prepare*

1. Start by making the bread pudding. When it is ready to go in the oven, begin preparing the pork. If you are going to serve the menu the day you prepare the bread pudding and the pork, peel and cut the carrots for the sautéed carrots while the cabbage is wilting. When the cabbage is ready, continue with the pork recipe. Once the pork is simmering on its own, begin cooking with the carrots. Wait to add the grated cheese until just before serving.

2. When you are ready to serve, slice the pork loin and finish the sauce (step 3 of the recipe). Put the pan with the carrots over high heat and finish them, following step 4 of the recipe. Serve the pork loin with the carrots on the side. Finish with the sliced bread pudding.

I FIND FLANK STEAK AN INEXPENSIVE and very tasty way to have steak. Roasted vegetables always go well with grilled meats, and you can substitute a green salad for the fruit if you prefer.

Grilled Flank Steak (page 148)

Oven-Roasted Vegetables (page 178)

Fresh Fruit

minutes to prepare 45

1. Prepare the vegetables and place them in the oven.

2. Light the grill. Wait about 10 minutes (or, if you are making a salad, prepare it now), then begin making the flank steak.

3. Serve the flank steak with the vegetables.

HERE IS A PERFECT MENU to restore one's body and spirit at the end of a cold and dreary winter day.

Celery Root and Potato Soup (page 54)

Meat Pie, "Pizza" Style (page 156)

Mixed Green Salad (page 184)

50 *minutes to prepare*

1. Prepare the meat pie. Before putting it in the oven, begin making the soup. When all the ingredients for the soup are in the pot and are simmering, place the meat pie in the oven.

2. Prepare the salad but do not dress it yet. Serve the soup as soon as it is ready. When the meat pie is done, remove it from the oven and set it aside until you have finished the soup. Dress the salad and serve it either after the meat pie or along with it on the side.

Elegant Sit-Down Menus

HERE IS AN ELEGANT AND SUBSTANTIAL MENU that is ideally suited to the autumn and winter months. It will be necessary to go back in the kitchen after the soup for about 10 minutes. Do not worry about going back and forth between the dining room and the kitchen. A break between courses is good for the digestion, not to mention the enjoyment of the meal.

Porcini Mushroom Soup (page 46)

Rack of Lamb Encrusted with Parmesan Cheese (page 142)

Zucchini Sautéed with Fresh Mint (page 163)

Mixed Green Salad (page 184)

Tiramisù (page 208)

2 *hours to prepare*

1. Make the tiramisù the day before.

2. On the day of the dinner, start with the soup. Once you reach step 5 of the soup recipe, prepare the lamb through step 4, while the soup is cooking.

3. While the lamb is in the oven, rinse and cut the zucchini and chop the garlic and parsley, then prepare the salad through step 3 of the recipe. Remove the soup from the heat when it is done.

4. When you take the lamb out of the oven the first time, set it aside and serve the soup, reheating it gently if necessary.

5. When you are ready to continue, begin making the zucchini. Once the zucchini are in the pan, roll the lamb racks in the bread crumb mixture and put them back in the oven (step 5 of the lamb recipe), leaving the lamb in for 1 to 2 extra minutes since it will have cooled slightly while it was out.

6. When everyone has finished the lamb and zucchini, dress the salad and serve it.

7. When you are ready to serve the dessert, take it out of the refrigerator, portion it onto dessert plates, and sprinkle some fresh cocoa on top of each serving.

HERE IS AN ELEGANT MENU that is certain to impress your guests. Most of it can be made several hours ahead of time, so that you will only need to be in the kitchen about 20 minutes before serving to prepare the tenderloin.

Tomato Soup (page 60)

Beef Tenderloin with Black Olives (page 145)

Sautéed Carrots with Marsala (page 161)

Chocolate and Amaretti Custard (page 206)

minutes to prepare 105

1. Make the chocolate and amaretti custard the day before, or at least 2 hours ahead of time.

2. Begin making the tomato soup. Once the soup is cooking, start the carrots. When they are tender and you have sautéed them until they have begun to brown, remove from the heat and set aside.

3. About 10 minutes before you plan on sitting down at the table, begin preparing the tenderloin. Cook the steaks, reducing the time by 2 minutes, then remove the meat and set it aside. Move the skillet off the heat and wait to add the wine until later.

4. Serve the soup, reheating it if necessary.

5. When you are ready to serve the tenderloin, place both the carrots and the skillet you cooked the tenderloin in over medium-high heat. When the carrots begin to sizzle, finish the recipe, adding the Marsala, flour, and parsley. As soon as the tenderloin skillet is hot, finish the recipe by adding the red wine and olives. Return the steaks to the pan, cover, lower the heat to medium, and allow them to heat through, about 1 to 2 minutes. Serve the steaks with the carrots.

6. End the meal with the chocolate amaretti custard.

HERE IS A QUICK AND ELEGANT seafood menu. The refreshing crunchy salad cleanses the palate and the luscious glazed peaches are a perfect light ending to the meal.

Linguine with Shrimp (page 78)

Red Snapper with Fresh Tomatoes and Black Olives (page 93)

Crunchy Salad (page 185)

Glazed Peaches in White Wine (page 214)

75 *minutes to prepare*

1. Begin by preparing the peaches. While they are poaching, make the sauce for the red snapper by following the recipe through step 4, then stir in the olives and capers, remove from the heat, and set aside. When the peaches are done, set them aside but do not refrigerate them.

2. Prepare the crunchy salad through step 4 of the recipe and set aside.

3. Approximately 30 minutes before you are ready to serve, begin making the pasta recipe. While the linguine is cooking, return the sauce for the fish to medium heat. Just before serving the pasta, put the fish fillets in and resume the recipe at step 5.

4. The salad can be served either as a side dish with the fish or afterward as a separate course. Either way, it should be dressed just before serving.

5. When it is time for dessert, serve the peaches with their juice.

HERE IS A VERY FINE and delicate menu made up entirely of seafood and ending with a refreshing orange tart. Practically everything can be prepared ahead of time so that the only time one has to be in the kitchen is for a few minutes to finish the shrimp sauce for the pasta. There are vegetables that cook with the fish, so a separate vegetable dish is not necessary, but if you wish, boiled new potatoes would go very well with the fish course.

Thinly Sliced Sea Bass Marinated in Lemon (page 40)

Linguine with Shrimp (page 78)

Fish Baked in Foil with Juniper Berries (page 102)

Sicilian Orange Tart (page 200)

minutes to prepare 80

1. Make the orange tart and the marinated sea bass at least 3 hours before serving, or even the day before. Begin with the orange tart. While the tart shell is baking, prepare the sea bass. Once the sea bass is done, make the orange filling, pour it into the shell, and finish baking the tart. Refrigerate the tart as soon as it is cool enough. It is fine to leave the sea bass out at room temperature up to 6 hours; if you make it the day before, you need to refrigerate it, but remember to take it out of the refrigerator at least 1 hour before serving.

2. Before your guests arrive, prepare the fish with juniper berries until it is ready to go into the oven and complete the pasta recipe through step 4. If you will be serving boiled new potatoes, prepare these now as well. Preheat the oven to 450°F.

3. Approximately 15 minutes before serving the appetizer, place the fish in the oven (if it is a delicate fish, such as halibut, wait 10 more minutes). Put on the water for the pasta. Reheat the sauce for the pasta and add the cream. Once the cream is reduced by half, remove the pan from the heat.

4. When the water for the pasta is boiling, salt it, put the linguine in, and serve the appetizer. After the linguine has cooked for about 8 minutes, return to the kitchen. Place the sauce over medium-high heat and put in the shrimp. When the pasta is ready, drain it, toss it with the sauce, and serve it at once. Meanwhile, check the fish for doneness by opening the foil slightly and testing the thickest part with a fork. When it is done, remove it from the oven and leave it in the sealed aluminum foil, where it will stay hot for up to 20 minutes. After the pasta, serve the fish, and the potatoes if desired. The orange tart is ready to serve as is, straight from the refrigerator.

EVEN THOUGH RISOTTO cannot be made ahead of time and requires constant stirring for 20 minutes, do not be discouraged from serving it when you are entertaining. I do it all the time. As long as your kitchen has enough room, your guests can easily be enticed to come and watch you, or even help stir!

Butternut Squash Risotto (page 80)

Pan-Roasted Veal Stuffed with Spinach (page 130)

Artichoke and Potato Casserole (page 170)

Mixed Green Salad (page 184)

Italian Apple Pie (page 198)

3 *hours to prepare*

1. Begin with the dessert. If you want to serve it chilled, it is best to make it the day before; otherwise, begin at least 3 hours before your guests arrive. Once the apples are cooking in the pan, you can begin working on the veal. If you are making it the same day, after you have added the tomatoes and the meat is simmering, begin preparing the artichoke and potato casserole; otherwise, wait until the day of the party to prepare the artichokes and potatoes as well as to complete steps 3 and 5 below. Once the casserole is assembled and covered with the aluminum foil, set it aside. Cook the veal until it is tender, then keep it in its cooking juices.

2. Make sure to check the apples and turn them from time to time.

3. Prepare the squash for the risotto (follow the recipe to the end of step 2).

4. When the apples are done and they have cooled down, finish making the apple pie.

5. Assemble the mixed salad but do not dress it.

6. About 30 minutes before you want to begin serving, preheat the oven to 400°F. Heat the broth for the risotto in a saucepan and once it comes to a boil, lower the heat to a gentle simmer. Reheat the squash. When the squash is hot, put in the rice and make the risotto. As soon as the oven is hot, put in the artichoke casserole. When it is done, turn the oven off but leave the casserole inside to keep it hot.

7. After you have served and eaten the risotto, remove the artichoke casserole from the oven. Put the roast on a cutting board and place the pan with the juices on the stove. If the sauce in the pan needs to be reduced, raise the heat until the sauce is thick enough to coat a spoon, then reduce the heat to very low. Cut the veal into slices about ½ inch thick. Place the slices in the sauce and turn them several times until they have heated through. This will take 3 to 4 minutes. Arrange the veal slices on a platter and pour the hot sauce over them. Serve along with the artichoke casserole.

8. Dress and serve the salad, and follow with the apple pie.

THIS IS AN INCREDIBLY EASY MENU to put together and serve. The preparation time is long only because the ossobuco needs to cook for at least 2 hours, but it does so with very little attention from the cook. Since both the veal shanks and the dessert are as good, if not better, the second day, I encourage you to make them the day before. The day of the party, all you need to do is make the pasta sauce and the gratinéed peppers, which should take only about half an hour to prepare.

Orecchiette with Fresh Tomato, Basil, and Ricotta Salata (page 75)

Sweet-and-Sour Braised Veal Shanks (page 132)

Gratinéed Red, Green, and Yellow Peppers (page 175)

Chocolate and Amaretti Custard (page 206)

3 *hours to prepare*

1. Make the ossobuco the day before. When it is done, do not reduce the liquid in the pan; in fact, if there is not very much left, add some water. Transfer to a container that will hold the shanks snugly in a single layer, add all the liquid in the pan, and refrigerate overnight. While the veal is cooking, make the custard.

2. Anytime during the day of the dinner, you can make the sauce for the pasta and get the peppers ready to go into the oven. Begin with the pasta sauce, and while the tomatoes are cooking, start preparing the peppers. When the tomatoes are done, remove from the heat and set aside until you are ready to cook the pasta. The peppers can be kept in the baking dish until it is time to bake them.

3. About 30 minutes before you want to serve the pasta, put on a pot of water for the pasta and preheat the oven to 450°F for the peppers. While you are waiting for the water to boil, put the ossobuco back into a pot. Cover and place over low heat. When the pasta water is boiling, add salt and put in the pasta. Reheat the tomato sauce over low heat and shave the ricotta salata. Put the peppers in the oven. (They will probably take a little longer than the pasta, so you will probably need to go back into the kitchen after serving the pasta to take them out.) When the pasta is cooked, toss it with the sauce and serve it with the cheese shavings.

4. After you have finished the pasta, transfer the veal shanks to a serving platter. Raise the heat under the pot to reduce the sauce, then pour it over the veal. Serve with the gratinéed peppers. Serve the chocolate amaretti custard straight from the refrigerator.

THIS ELEGANT SEAFOOD MENU is very easy to prepare. Everything can be done ahead of time except for sautéing the fish.

Stuffed Squid with Chickpea Sauce (page 38)

Halibut Fillets Sautéed with Leeks and Red Peppers (page 90)

Cauliflower Gratin with Tomato and Fresh Sheep's Milk Cheese (page 176)

Amaretto Cookie Frozen Dessert (page 211)

minutes to prepare, plus 20 minutes for the dessert the day before 75

1. Make the *semifreddo* the day before and place it in the freezer.

2. At any time the day of the dinner but at least 1 hour before your guests arrive, begin making the stuffed squid. Once they are in the pot cooking, begin preparing the cauliflower. While the tomatoes are reducing, start the sauce for the fish. When the leeks and peppers are done, set them aside. Proceed with the cauliflower recipe until the baking pan is ready to go into the oven.

3. About 15 minutes before you are ready to serve, preheat the oven to 375°F for the cauliflower. If you wish to reheat the squid, place the pot they are in over medium heat and allow to simmer for 3 to 4 minutes. Make the chickpea sauce while they are reheating. Take the stuffed squid out of their poaching liquid and slice them. Pour some of the sauce over the slices, put the rest in a sauceboat, and serve. Before joining your guests, put the cauliflower in the oven.

4. After the squid course, return to the kitchen to cook the fish, proceeding with step 5 of the recipe. Don't forget to take the cauliflower out of the oven when it is ready. It is fine to let it stand until you finish the fish. When ready, serve the halibut and the cauliflower. (You may want to set a separate small plate for the cauliflower so the fish juices do not get mixed in with it.)

5. When it is time for dessert, remove the *semifreddo* from the freezer and unmold, slice, and serve it.

HERE IS A COMPLETELY VEGETARIAN MENU that is elegant and easy to put together.

Crostini with Tomatoes and Arugula (page 35)

Fusilli with Cauliflower and Black Olives (page 70)

Tricolor Vegetable Casserole (page 180)

Coffee-Flavored Frozen Dessert with Warm Chocolate Sauce (page 212)

85 *minutes to prepare, plus 25 minutes for the dessert the day before*

1. Make the dessert the day before. You can also make the chocolate sauce, as it will keep for several days in the refrigerator.

2. At any time during the day of the party, but at least 1¼ hours before your guests arrive, assemble the vegetable casserole and set it aside. Make the sauce for the pasta through step 6 and set aside.

3. About 25 minutes before your guests arrive, make the crostini. When done, reduce the oven temperature to 400°F. I suggest serving the crostini as an hors d'oeuvre before sitting down at the table.

4. Approximately 30 minutes before you wish to serve the pasta, put a pot of water on to boil and place the vegetable casserole in the oven. When the water boils, salt it, put in the fusilli, and gently reheat the sauce. When it begins simmering, add the olives, stir for a couple of minutes, and remove it from the heat. When the pasta is cooked, drain it and toss with the sauce, adding the grated pecorino cheese. Serve at once, and don't forget to take the vegetable casserole out of the oven when it is done. It is fine for it to stand until you are ready to serve it after the pasta.

5. While the casserole is being served, place the chocolate sauce in a double boiler to reheat. When you are ready to serve the dessert, take it out of the freezer, slice it, place a slice on each dessert plate, pour some chocolate sauce on top, and serve.

Buffet and Picnic Menus

HERE IS A RUSTIC, HEARTY BUFFET that will satisfy the hungriest appetite while providing enough variety to appeal to the casual grazer. The marinated fruit is a refreshing finish to the rich dishes that precede it, and the chocolates will appease any sweet tooth without adding a heavy dessert to the buffet.

Red Cabbage Slaw (page 191)

Baked Ham-and-Cheese Rice Casserole (page 86)

Veal Stew with Green and Yellow Peppers (page 128)

Summer Salad with Baked Red Onions (page 188)

Mixed Fruit Marinated with Kirsch (page 215)

Chocolate Puffs (page 217)

2 *hours to prepare*

1. The day before or at least several hours before the party, make the chocolate puffs.

2. Begin preparing the rest of the food at least 2 hours before you plan on serving it. First, preheat the oven to 400°F. Make the fruit salad and place it in the refrigerator. Bake the onions for the summer salad. While the onions are baking, cook the eggs for the summer salad and make the veal stew through step 3. Assemble the rice casserole but do not bake it yet. Prepare the red cabbage slaw and set it aside without adding the dressing. When the veal is tender, add the peppers and cook them, but hold the cream until just before serving.

3. About 30 minutes before you are ready to serve, preheat the oven to 400°F. When the oven is hot, put the rice casserole in the oven and bake as directed. Reheat the veal stew if necessary and add the cream. Assemble the summer salad, omitting the tuna, and make the dressing. Dress the red cabbage slaw with the salt, oil, and vinegar. When the rice casserole is ready, bring everything out except for the fruit and the chocolates, which you will serve together later for dessert.

HERE IS A COLD BUFFET that is perfect for summer. The turkey breast recipe is usually served hot, but I have found it also to be delicious at room temperature. If wonderful fresh fruit is available, serve it at the end with the dessert. I recommend making the orange tart and the marinated sea bass the day before so you will have less to do the day of the party.

Thinly Sliced Sea Bass Marinated in Lemon (page 40)

Tuna and Italian Rice Salad (page 192)

Turkey Breast Fillets with Lemon and Olives (page 126)

Mrs. Torti's Zucchini (page 165)

Sicilian Orange Tart (page 200)

minutes to prepare 80

1. Make the orange tart the day before, or at least 3 to 4 hours before serving, so that it has time to chill. While the crust is baking, begin preparing the marinated sea bass. Finish assembling the fish appetizer as the tart bakes.

2. Make the turkey recipe. When it is finished, let the fillets steep in their sauce.

3. Begin making the tuna and rice salad. Once the eggs, the red pepper, and the olives are ready and you are waiting for the rice to finish cooking, start the zucchini recipe.

4. When you are ready to serve, bring everything out (except for the orange tart) to come to room temperature. When your guests are ready for dessert, serve the orange tart, along with some fresh fruit, if desired.

THIS IS AN ENTIRELY MEATLESS BUFFET where everything except for the potatoes can be served at room temperature.

Tomatoes, Green Beans, Yellow Peppers, and Tuna in a Mustard Dressing (page 194)

Grilled Mushrooms with Balsamic Vinegar (page 36)

Poached Fish with a Savory Green Sauce (page 97)

Spinach Loaf (page 179)

Potatoes Stewed with Onions and Tomatoes (page 168)

Rum and Strawberry Layer Cake (page 207)

90 *total minutes to prepare, plus 20 minutes for the dessert the day before*

1. Make the dessert at least 3 hours before the party or even the day before.

2. Preheat the oven to 350°F. Cook the spinach for the spinach loaf and leave it in a colander to drain. While the spinach is cooking, start the potato recipe. Once the potatoes and tomatoes are on, finish making the spinach loaf. When the potatoes are done, set them aside.

3. Put two pots of water on to boil: one for the green beans and one with the onion and carrot in it for the fish. Trim the beans and put them in the pot once the water is boiling and salted. Prepare the peppers and tomatoes as directed in step 3 of the green bean salad recipe. Once the water for the fish is boiling, add the salt and vinegar and put in the fish. Make the sauce for the fish and put it aside in a sauceboat. When the fish is done, take it out, place it on a serving platter, and cover it with plastic wrap. When the green beans are done, you can mix them with all the ingredients for the salad including the dressing, but not the salt. Check to see whether the spinach loaf in the oven is ready.

4. Make the grilled mushrooms. If you want to serve these warm, do not start them until your guests arrive.

5. When you are ready to serve, reheat the potatoes over medium-low heat. In the meantime, toss the green bean salad and adjust for salt. You can bring everything out at once except for the dessert.

HERE IS AN ELEGANT SPECIAL-OCCASION PICNIC. It undoubtedly takes longer to prepare than slapping together a ham-and-cheese sandwich, but it is also infinitely more rewarding. A good bottle of white wine, chilled if possible, is a highly recommended accompaniment.

Tuna and Italian Rice Salad (page 192)

Poached Fish with a Savory Green Sauce (page 97)

Spinach Loaf (page 179)

Lemon-Scented Almond Cookies (page 216)

minutes to prepare 90

1. Make the almond cookies the day before or even several days in advance.

2. Place three pots of water on to boil: one for the rice, one for the eggs, and one for the fish. Rinse the spinach for the spinach loaf, and if you have enough room on the stove, cook the spinach. Preheat the oven to 350°F.

3. Make the sauce for the fish and put it in a spillproof container. Cook the fish and let it cool on a plate when it is done.

4. Assemble and bake the spinach torte. Let it cool completely, then slice it.

5. Once the rice has been cooked and rinsed, assemble the rice salad but wait to dress it until just before serving (or just before leaving the house if you're picnicking).

THE FRESH FLAVORS and contrasting textures of these items will make a delicious picnic.

Italian Open-Faced Omelet with Scallions (page 41)

Chicken Salad with Pomegranate, Pine Nuts, and Raisins (page 196)

Crunchy Salad (page 185)

60 *minutes to prepare*

1. Begin by cooking the chicken for the chicken salad. While it is cooking, prepare the frittata. When the chicken is done, which will be before the frittata is, set it aside to cool. Once the frittata is cooked, let it cool and then cut it into wedges approximately 1 inch thick.

2. Make the crunchy salad but do not dress it. Instead, mix the salt, lemon juice, and olive oil together and put it in a spillproof container. When ready to serve, pour the dressing over the salad and toss well.

3. Assemble the chicken salad last. Dress it just before you leave the house, and it will be fine for several hours.

Index

fontina, grilled chicken breast
    stuffed with asparagus
    and, 112–13
fricco di agnello alla cernaia, 143
frittata alle cipolline, 41
frozen dessert:
    amaretto cookie, 211
    coffee-flavored, with warm
        chocolate sauce, 212–13
fruit marinated with kirsch,
    mixed, 215
frutta mista al kirsch, 215
*funghi ai ferri alla moda dei
    porcini,* 162
*funghi ai ferri all' aceto
    balsamico,* 36
fusilli ai porri e salsiccia,
    72–73
fusilli al cavolfiore e olive,
    70–71
fusilli:
    with cauliflower and black
        olives, 70–71
    with sausage and leeks,
        72–73

G
gamberi coi fagioli, 106
gamberi del diavolo, i, 104
gamberoni al forno, 105
garlic, 22
    pan-roasted pompano fil-
        lets with rosemary and,
        92
gelato di ananas, 210
glazed peaches in white wine,
    214
granchi in graticola, 107
grapes, sautéed pork chops
    with, 135
gratin, apple and pear, 204
green beans:
    with fresh tomatoes and
        ham, 172
    marinated, 190

green beans *(cont.)*
    tomatoes, yellow peppers
        and tuna in a mustard
        dressing, 194–95
green sauce, savory, poached
    fish with, 97

H
halibut fillets sautéed with
    leeks and red peppers,
    90–91
ham:
    -and-cheese rice casserole,
        baked, 86–87
    green beans with fresh
        tomatoes and, 172
herbs, 23

I
ice cream, pineapple, 210
insalata caprese, 187
insalata croccante, 185
insalata di cavolo nero,
    191
insalata di cipolle al forno,
    188–89
*insalata di funghi, rucola, e
    parmigiano,* 186
*insalata di pollo col
    melograno,* 196
insalata di riso e tonno, 192
insalata di tonno e fagiolini,
    194–95
insalata mista, 184
Italian apple pie, 198–99
Italian open-faced omelet
    with scallions, 41
Italian pantry, 19–23

J
juniper berries:
    fish baked in foil with,
        102–3
    slow-cooked beef with,
        149

K
knives, sharpening of, 27

L
lamb:
    braised, with an egg and
        lemon glaze, 144
    chops, grilled, with a lemon
        and vinegar sauce, 141
    rack of, encrusted with
        Parmesan cheese, 142
    shoulder braised with
        tomatoes, 143
leeks:
    fusilli with sausage and,
        72–73
    halibut fillets sautéed with
        red peppers and, 90–91
lemon:
    and egg glaze, braised lamb
        with, 144
    -scented almond cookies,
        216
    thinly sliced sea bass mari-
        nated in, 40
    turkey breast fillets with
        olive and, 126
    and vinegar sauce, lamb
        chops grilled with, 141
linguine ai gamberi,
    78–79
linguine with shrimp,
    78–79
liver, calf's, with raisins and
    onions, 134

M
manzo al latte, 150
Marsala:
    fresh tuna steaks with
        mushrooms and, 98–99
    sautéed carrots with, 161
    sautéed
meat, 109–57
    broth, homemade, 45

petti di pollo alla campagnola,
	114–15
petti di pollo alla Guido Reni,
	112–13
petti di pollo arrotolati, 118
petti di pollo tricolore,
	110–11
petto di tacchino alle olive,
	126
pie, Italian apple, 198–99
pineapple ice cream, 210
pine nuts, chicken salad with
	pomegranate, raisins and,
	196
"pizza" di carne, 156–57
pollo ai porcini secchi,
	122–23
pollo al chianti, 119
pollo alle olive verdi, 120–21
pollo al pomodoro e olive,
	124–25
polpettine in brodo, 58
polpettone saporito, 154–55
pomegranate, chicken salad
	with pine nuts, raisins
	and, 196
pompano al rosmarino,
	92
pompano fillets, pan-roasted,
	with rosemary and garlic,
	92
porcini mushroom(s):
	chicken braised with,
		122–23
	chicken breast fillets with,
		116–17
	dried, 21
	mashed potatoes, 169
	rustic soup with chickpeas
		and, 55
	soup, 46–47
pork:
	loin braised with Savoy
		cabbage, 137–38
	sausage, homemade, 49

pork chops:
	with fresh fennel, 136
	sautéed, with grapes, 135
portobello mushrooms,
	grilled, porcini style, 162
potato(es):
	and artichoke casserole,
		170–71
	and celery root soup, 54
	porcini mashed, 169
	stewed with onions and
		tomatoes, 168
	and wild mushroom soup,
		52–53
pot roast braised with butter-
	nut squash, 151
pudding:
	almond bread, 202–3
	chocolate ricotta, 205
puré di patate ai porcini, 169

R

raisins:
	calf's liver with onions and,
		134
	chicken salad with pome-
		granate, pine nuts and,
		196
red and yellow pepper risotto,
	82–83
red cabbage slaw, 191
red snapper with fresh toma-
	toes and black olives, 93
red wine, chicken braised
	with, 119
ribollita, la, 50–51
rice, 20, 80–88
	casserole, baked ham-and-
		cheese, 86–87
	Italian, and tuna salad, 192
ricotta chocolate pudding,
	205
ricotta salata, orecchiette
	with fresh tomato, basil
	and, 75

riso al forno, 86–87
risotto:
	butternut squash, 80–81
	red and yellow pepper,
		82–83
	with shrimp and asparagus,
		84–85
	the un-, 88
risotto ai peperoni e
	pomodoro fresco, 82–83
risotto al profumo di zucca,
	80–81
risotto coi gamberi e asparagi,
	84–85
risotto finto, 88
rosemary:
	chicken breast fillets rolled
		with pancetta, sage and,
		118
	pan-roasted pompano
		fillets with garlic and, 92
	shrimp broiled with, 105
	Tuscan beans with toma-
		toes and, 173
rum and strawberry layer
	cake, 207

S

sage:
	beef stew with cannellini
		beans and, 152–53
	chicken breast fillets rolled
		with pancetta, rosemary
		and, 118
	-scented grilled veal chops,
		127
salads, 183–96
	chicken, with pomegran-
		ate, pine nuts, and
		raisins, 196
	crunchy, 185
	marinated green beans, 190
	mixed green, 184
	mushroom, arugula, and
		Parmesan, 186

tomato(es):
    basil, and bread salad,
        193
    canned, 20
    cauliflower gratin with
        fresh sheep's milk cheese
        and, 176–77
    chicken braised with black
        olives and, 124–25
    crostini with arugula and,
        35
    fresh tuna, arugula and, 34
    green beans, yellow
        peppers, and tuna in a
        mustard dressing, 194–95
    lamb shoulder braised with,
        143
    mozzarella and basil salad,
        187
    plum, peeling of, 24
    potatoes stewed with
        onions and, 168
    soup, 60
    spaghetti with anchovies
        and, 65
    spaghetti with onions and,
        64
    Tuscan beans with rose-
        mary and, 173
    zucchini sautéed with
        onions and, 164
tomatoes, fresh:
    clam soup with, 61
    devil's shrimp with brandy
        and, 104
    green beans with ham and,
        172
    orecchiette with basil,
        ricotta salata and, 75
    red snapper with black
        olives and, 93
    thin spaghetti with egg-
        plant, mozzarella and,
        66–67

tomato sauce, simple, savory
    three-meat loaf with,
    154–55
*tonno fresco al Marsala e
    funghi,* 98–99
tonno fresco e rucola, 34
torta di mele, 198–99
torta di spinaci, 179
tuna:
    fresh, arugula and tomato,
        34
    and Italian rice salad,
        192
    steaks, fresh, with Marsala
        and mushrooms, 98–99
    tomatoes, green beans and
        yellow peppers in a mus-
        tard dressing, 194–95
turkey breast fillets with
    lemon and olive, 126
Tuscan beans with tomatoes
    and rosemary, 173
Tuscan vegetable soup,
    classic, 50–51

U
un-risotto, the, 88

V
veal:
    chops, sage-scented grilled,
        127
    pan-roasted, stuffed with
        spinach, 130–31
    shanks, sweet-and-sour
        braised, 132–33
    stew with green and yellow
        peppers, 128–29
vegetable(s), 159–81
    casserole, tricolor, 180–81
    oven-roasted, 178
    soup, classic Tuscan, 50–51
    see also specific vegetables
verdure al forno, 178

vinegar and lemon sauce,
    lamb chops grilled with,
    141

W
"wedded" soup, 56–57
white wine, glazed peaches in,
    214
wild mushroom and potato
    soup, 52–53
wines, 23
    beef tenderloin braised in
        three, 146
    see also red wine; white wine

Z
zucchine alla menta, 163
*zucchine al pomodoro e
    cipolle,* 164
*zucchine della Signora Torti,
    le,* 165
zucchine ripiene, 166–67
zucchini:
    Mrs. Torti's, 165
    sautéed with fresh mint,
        163
    sautéed with onions and
        tomatoes, 164
    spaghetti alla carbonara
        with, 68–69
    stuffed with ground beef
        and mozzarella, 166–67
zuppa campagnola, 55
zuppa con funghi e patate,
    52–53
zuppa di fagioli e scarola,
    44
zuppa di pomodoro, 60
zuppa di verza e salsiccia,
    48
zuppa di vongole, 61

Index of Recipes
That Can Be Made Ahead